Rapid Ethnographies

Rapid ethnographies are used in a wide range of fields to speed up research quickly and effectively. This book is the first practical guide to rapid ethnographies, helping readers to improve skills in the design, implementation, dissemination and use of findings generated through rapid ethnographic research. It gives advice and guidelines for carrying out rapid and rigorous research and provides details of tools used in the field. Vignettes reflecting on the author's research are included throughout, including observations on research carried out during the COVID-19 pandemic, to highlight how challenges of conducting rapid ethnographies can be overcome. Case studies across a range of subjects are also included, to demonstrate how rapid ethnographies can be applied in practice. With its useful tools and easy-to-read format, it will be used by teachers and students, as well as researchers wanting to successfully implement rapid ethnographies in their own work.

Cecilia Vindrola-Padros is a medical anthropologist who co-directs the Rapid Research Evaluation and Appraisal Lab (RREAL) at University College London, UK. She works across various interdisciplinary teams, using rapid ethnographies, rapid appraisals and rapid evaluations to study and improve healthcare delivery in the UK and abroad.

D1451818

Rapid Ethnographies
A Practical Guide

Cecilia Vindrola-Padros

University College London

CAMBRIDGE
UNIVERSITY PRESS

CAMBRIDGE
UNIVERSITY PRESS

University Printing House, Cambridge CB2 8BS, United Kingdom

One Liberty Plaza, 20th Floor, New York, NY 10006, USA

477 Williamstown Road, Port Melbourne, VIC 3207, Australia

314–321, 3rd Floor, Plot 3, Splendor Forum, Jasola District Centre, New Delhi – 110025, India

79 Anson Road, #06–04/06, Singapore 079906

Cambridge University Press is part of the University of Cambridge.

It furthers the University's mission by disseminating knowledge in the pursuit of education, learning, and research at the highest international levels of excellence.

www.cambridge.org
Information on this title: www.cambridge.org/9781108493369
DOI: 10.1017/9781108623568

First published 2021

A catalogue record for this publication is available from the British Library.

Library of Congress Cataloging-in-Publication Data
Names: Vindrola-Padros, Cecilia, 1983- author.
Title: Rapid ethnographies : a practical guide / Cecilia Vindrola.
Description: Cambridge ; New York, NY : Cambridge University Press, 2020. | Includes
    bibliographical references and index.
Identifiers: LCCN 2020021027 (print) | LCCN 2020021028 (ebook) | ISBN 9781108493369
    (hardback) | ISBN 9781108736992 (paperback) | ISBN 9781108623568 (epub)
Subjects: LCSH: Ethnology–Research–Methodology. | Ethnology–Fieldwork.
Classification: LCC GN345 .V56 2020 (print) | LCC GN345 (ebook) | DDC 305.80072/1–dc23
LC record available at https://lccn.loc.gov/2020021027
LC ebook record available at https://lccn.loc.gov/2020021028

ISBN 978-1-108-49336-9 Hardback
ISBN 978-1-108-73699-2 Paperback

To my boys (big and small)

Contents

Figures and Tables

Figure

Tables

Vignettes

Case Studies

1 Introduction

A few years ago, I attended a small symposium focused on the use of ethnographic research to explore cancer care. It was organised at a well-known university in the UK and was attended by experienced academics (anthropologists and other social scientists) working on cancer in the UK and abroad. I was asked to be a part of the discussion panel in the last session of the day. Since the goal of the panel was to bring together the main themes that had emerged during the day, I wanted to provide my reflections on the current state of ethnographic research on cancer and propose ways to take it forward.

One of my reflections was that ethnographic cancer research tends to be divorced from the realities of those who could use the findings. I talked about the benefits of ethnography, the additional layers of knowledge generated by this approach, its insight, its commitment to the value of human thought and experience. My argument was that these findings, these additional layers of meaning, were often left in articles or books and were not being used to improve the services patients received, the support provided to carers or the work conditions of staff delivering care. I then went on to explain how anthropologists working in more applied settings were developing approaches such as rapid ethnography and collaborative ethnography. As I mentioned these terms, I could see expressions around the room change. I continued to talk about the need to involve other stakeholders from initial stages of study design, to understand how they might view cancer care and see if any of the findings of the study would be useful to them. This led to a bit of murmuring.

My brief presentation then queried the way in which we share the findings in ethnographic research: Could we be doing this as the study is ongoing, could we share the findings in accessible ways? These questions led to some angry faces in the audience. Needless to say, several hands went up to ask questions straight after I finished talking. After a few minutes of heated discussion with quite senior academics (I was a research fellow at the time), I concluded that I would not be coming out of that room with any form of agreement or even an 'agree to disagree' stance in relation to ways in which we could make ethnographic research more timely and accessible. Had I proposed something so radical to generate this type of response? Why did my proposal to do this type of research make so many anthropologists feel uncomfortable?

I wasn't oblivious to the fact that the term 'rapid ethnography' was considered contradictory by some anthropologists who define ethnography in relation to the long-term engagement with a particular 'field'. Ethnographic research and fieldwork have changed so much since our traditional Malinowskian past that I did not expect such a rigid response from the audience. We are used to reading about multi-sited ethnography, mobile ethnography, virtual ethnography, auto-ethnography and even fiction ethnography, all with different coverages of spaces, time, materiality and aspects of the imagination.

The questions from the audience also alluded to concerns about producing ethnographic research with others. If the ethnography is co-produced, is the voice of the ethnographer censored in some way?, I was asked. There were interesting dynamics about the authority over social realities and authority over the text emerging. My reply went along the lines of: Isn't this authority always negotiated, even if we do not explicitly co-produce our ethnographies? The audience was not interested in seeing beyond the potential 'dangers' of doing ethnography rapidly or collaboratively.

Had I hit a nerve? Was there something about disciplinary identity here? If we reduce the time-frame of ethnography, if we change ethnography in its 'purist' form, then everyone will be able to do it. If everyone can do it, what will be our role as anthropologists in the production of knowledge? There was a hint of defensiveness in some of the comments, but what had I attacked? Or better yet, what were they defending?

My reflection and obsessive dissection of the events that transpired that day allowed me to see that the proposal of doing rapid ethnography could potentially pose deeper questions about what ethnography is. If ethnography is not defined by the amount of time one spends in the field, then what makes a study ethnographic? What is (or should be) the purpose of the work we do? What is our responsibility towards those who share their time and stories with us? If we are able to share findings at times when these can be used to inform decision-making processes, then shouldn't it be our responsibility to do so? In addition to introducing you to the vast landscape of rapid ethnographies, these are the questions I deal with throughout the book. Hopefully you can help me find some of the answers.

Timeliness and Research

Timeliness has been highlighted as a factor influencing the utility of research and evaluation findings in healthcare (McNall et al. 2004; Nunns 2009). As I was putting the finishing touches on this book, our world was dealing with the impact of the COVID-19 pandemic. My editing days were shaped by a country on lockdown, hundreds of daily deaths and requests from colleagues and healthcare authorities to assist with the development of rapid research to capture much-needed qualitative data to inform response efforts. Rapid research approaches and the expertise of our research team (the Rapid Research Evaluation and Appraisal Lab, RREAL) never felt more relevant.

Even beyond the context of global pandemics, only research findings shared at time points when they are able to inform decision-making will be able to produce improvements in care (Kilo 1998; Reed and Card 2016; Etchells et al. 2016). This has prompted the development of a wide range of rapid research approaches that aim to make findings available when they are most needed (McNall and Foster-Fishman 2007). These approaches are characterised by the short duration of research, use of multiple methods for data collection and teams of researchers, formative research designs where findings are fed back while the research is ongoing, and the development of actionable findings (adequate for purpose) to inform changes in policy and/or practice (McNall and Foster-Fishman 2007; Anker et al. 1993; Beebe 1995, 2014).

In the UK, the interest in rapid approaches to research has become more evident, with greater emphasis placed on the need for timely findings and rapid, relevant and responsive research. The National Institute for Health Research (NIHR) has recently funded two rapid service evaluation teams (called RSET and BRACE) that aim to reduce the amount of time involved in setting up national service evaluations. I have been involved in the development of an additional center in the UK called the Rapid Research, Evaluation and Appraisal Lab (RREAL), which seeks to expand and improve the use of rapid research approaches in healthcare through an intensive training programme, support during research design and implementation, and the development of rapid research to test out new approaches and methods.

The Center for Medicare and Medicaid Innovation in the US has created a Rapid Cycle Evaluation Group to test new payment and service delivery models and inform decisions at a policy and practice level in a timely manner (Shrank 2013). This shift towards rapid research is mirrored globally by transnational organisations such as the WHO, with their development of methods for rapid evidence synthesis to inform decision-making and the design of rapid advice guidelines for public health emergencies (Tricco et al. 2017; Garritty et al. 2017).

The field of rapid research has advanced considerably in the last few decades and now covers a large number of techniques and approaches (i.e. rapid appraisals, rapid ethnographic assessments [REA], rapid qualitative inquiry [RQI], rapid assessment procedures [RAPs], rapid assessment, response and evaluation [RARE], and quick, focused or short-term ethnographies). Rapid evaluation methods have also been developed in the form of real time evaluations (RTE), rapid feedback evaluations (RFE), rapid evaluation methods (REM) and rapid-cycle evaluations.

One approach that has become increasingly popular is rapid ethnography. Rapid ethnographies are informed by theories and methods used in conventional, more long-term ethnographies, but seek to deliver findings over shorter periods of time. Rapid ethnographies emerged in the 1980s and have diversified to include a wide range of approaches for conducting ethnographic research as a lone researcher or in teams. Proponents of rapid ethnographies have argued that rich ethnographic data and meaningful engagement with field sites can be achieved in shorter studies as long as ethnographers are able to develop mechanisms for intensive fieldwork, a different (more targeted or focused) delineation of the field, and strategies for collaboration (with participants or other researchers) (Handwerker 2001; Knoblauch 2005; Pink and Morgan 2013; Wall 2014). A recent review we carried out on the use of rapid ethnographies in healthcare showed a notable increase in the use of rapid ethnographies in the last five years and their expansion beyond the social sciences (now becoming more popular in nursing and medicine) (Vindrola-Padros and Vindrola-Padros 2018).

Even though rapid ethnographies are now widely used in the social sciences and beyond, their expansion has not gone uncontested. Some authors have argued that the use of the 'ethnography label' poses potential risks for rapid ethnographies, where researchers might sacrifice the use of theory for the sake of brevity, fostering an instrumental and acritical research approach (Culpit et al. 2018). Others have also argued that rapid ethnographies are not ethnographies at all and need to be named differently to avoid confusion with terminology (Beebe 2004). In these cases, shorter study time frames are inextricably associated with lower quality of research, not capable of developing the insight and understanding conventional ethnographies are able to produce. As a consequence, rapid ethnographies are often represented as a 'quick and dirty' exercise (Pink and Morgan 2013; Vindrola-Padros and Vindrola-Padros 2018).

The aim of this book is to present a critical overview and analysis of the use of rapid ethnographies. I have designed the book to provide a detailed description of how different rapid ethnographic approaches have been used in the past, critically analysing their use, but also highlighting their potential. As an applied medical anthropologist who has carried out health-based research in several countries over the years and has supervised graduate and post-graduate students in different fields, I have become convinced that rapid ethnographies, if designed and implemented properly, can make important contributions to our study of social phenomena, while helping to inform changes in policy and practice. Rapid ethnographies can also help question research designs used in conventional ethnographic approaches by testing underlying assumptions on the relationship between time spent in the field, the building of relationships and the production of knowledge. In many ways, rapid ethnographies can lead to a basic question: If ethnography is not defined by the length of time in the field, then what makes a study ethnographic? Even though this book is an introduction to rapid ethnographies, this question, concerning all ethnographic research, will feature prominently throughout the chapters.

What Are Rapid Ethnographies?

Ethnographies propose a way of thinking and a way of being-in-the world that is quite different from other perspectives. Ethnographers seek to see and understand the world through the eyes of others, by participating actively in their daily lives. They tend to combine different methods to explore the particularities of thought and practice, developing rich layers of insight into human experiences (Watson 2011). The detail of the everyday, obtained by an immersion in the context of research and active participation in the lives of others, is used as a window into the particularities of the locale, but also as a connection to other relevant scales (van Maanen 1996; 2011). Ethnographies maintain a multi-scalar view, where through the analysis of the local, they are able to capture processes operating at other, more abstract, and perhaps more global levels (Xiang 2013; Tsing 2005).

Ethnographies have also been characterised for their conceptual openness. According to Dalakoglou and Harvey (2012), ethnographies are able to locate material and social relations without needing to decide in advance on the ontology, the scale or the extension of such relationships. In other words, ethnographies rely on the ethnographer's capacity to be surprised, to encounter the unexpected. Rivoal and Salazar (2013) have argued that a key characteristic of the ethnographic method is serendipity, or 'the art of making an unsought finding' (Van Andel 1994: 631). This requires approaching the field with a critical reflection of one's own preconceptions and undergoing a continuous exercise of self-reflection to ensure openness to ways of thinking and behaving that might not have been expected. As Olivier de Sardan (1995: 77) has argued, 'anthropologists are trained to observe what they are not prepared to see.'

Ethnographies also promote the decentering of analysis, through their focus on reflexivity, where a dynamic relationship is acknowledged between one's own positionality and the locality and mobility of the topics, people and things under analysis (Osterlund-Potzch 2017). This dynamic relationship is constantly negotiated by the ethnographer, participants and the fieldsite and permeates all levels of ethnographic interpretation.

Traditionally, ethnographic research has relied on extensive periods of fieldwork (Marcus and Faubion 2009). As Beebe (2004: 3) has argued, 'the case for prolonged fieldwork advanced by anthropologists [. . .] is based on tradition and the argument that it takes time to develop intellectualized competence in another culture, to be accepted, to develop rapport, to be included in gossip, and to get information about social change.' Other authors have queried this long-standing assumption, arguing that the traditional long periods of fieldwork in anthropological doctoral training are continuously reconfigured to adapt to the context where the research will take place, the needs and inclinations of the researcher and more general trends in anthropological thought and practice (Marcus and Faubion 2009). These authors have also sought to unpack what we mean by fieldwork, highlighting instances where the researcher is not physically in the field (i.e. in a library, archive or discussing with colleagues at their university) but is still carrying out research that constitutes fieldwork (Marcus and Faubion 2009).

Developments in the field of rapid ethnographies have also questioned equating ethnography with long-term research (Pink and Morgan 2013). There is an evident time issue when defining rapid ethnographies, but what are the other features of this type of design? Definitions of rapid ethnographies vary. In a recent review of the use of rapid ethnographies in healthcare (Vindrola-Padros and Vindrola-Padros 2018), we found at least five different labels associated with rapid ethnographic research (quick ethnography, focused ethnography, rapid ethnographic assessment, RARE and short-term ethnography). After reviewing these definitions and the ways in which the rapid ethnographies were designed, we proposed a working definition that could envelop all of these approaches into one genre. Rapid ethnographies were defined in relation to the following characteristics: (1) the research was carried out over a short, compressed or intensive period of time; (2) the research captured relevant social, cultural and behavioural information and focused on human experiences and practices; (3) the research engaged with anthropological and other social science theories and promoted reflexivity; (4) data were collected from multiple sources and triangulated during analysis; and (5) more than one field researcher was used to save time and cross-check data (Vindrola-Padros and Vindrola-Padros 2018). We also argued that rapid ethnographies needed to be transparent and include detailed reporting of the design and implementation of this study. This was in response to the low quality of reporting we found in the articles included in the review, which we will discuss later on in the book.

The first characteristic included in our working definition creates problems for many researchers, as there is no consensus on what we mean by rapid, short, compressed or intensive periods of time. Whilst some authors suggest that the entire research process (from design to dissemination) should take place in less than six weeks for some rapid studies (Beebe 2005) and ninety days for rapid ethnographies (Handwerker 2001), recent literature reviews have highlighted variability for both, with study duration including three weeks (Pearson et al. 1989), seven weeks (Wilson and Kimane 1990), or two to three months (Bentley et al. 1988). In this book, I use a time frame of five days to six months to define rapid ethnographies on the basis of recently reported evidence (Vindrola-Padros and Vindrola-Padros 2018), with a view to capturing a wide spectrum of rapid ethnographic designs. I also cover examples of longer ethnographies that have designed rapid feedback loops for disseminating findings as I think these share some design characteristics with rapid ethnographies.

Vignette: When research needs to be rapid

Many years ago, I was approached by a senior manager in a children's hospital who was looking for a research team to evaluate a new service he had implemented in the hospital. The purpose of the new service was to provide some of the care required by patients as an outpatient service, reducing the need of children and their parents to travel to the hospital. A few months after the service had been rolled out, it was not providing care to the numbers of patients that had originally been estimated. This low number of patient cases was mainly due to staff members' unwillingness and inability to refer patients to the service.

I was asked to put together a team to carry out a diagnostic study to identify the main reasons why staff were not referring patients to the service. The caveat was that important decisions would need to be made about continuing or discontinuing the service at the next board meeting. This meant findings would need to be delivered in two months. From my point of view, this meant I would need to assemble a team, design a study protocol, collect data, analyse it and disseminate it in a user-friendly way in less than eight weeks.

It was not an easy process, but we managed to carry out a rapid appraisal of the main barriers to referral. We carried out interviews with staff, observed referral processes and the delivery of care in the outpatients area and carried out documentary analysis. We developed a visual summary of the findings (similar to an infographic) and shared it by the deadline. The board decided to continue with the service with the condition that the service leads develop action plans to address each of the referral barriers we had identified in our appraisal. The main changes that needed to be made were the development of better educational materials for hospital staff on what services the outpatient clinic could provide, the simplification of the paperwork required to refer patients (as some staff found this to be too time consuming) and the creation of a follow-up system where staff who referred patients to the outpatient service would be informed about these patients' outcomes after they were seen in outpatients.

Why Do We Need Rapid Ethnographies?

Over thirty years ago, Scrimshaw and Hurtado (1988: 97) asked an insightful question: 'must one spend a year in the field collecting ethnographic data in order to make useful recommendations for a health program?' Their question emerged out of an honest desire to use ethnographic research to inform the design and delivery of interventions aimed at improving the healthcare of communities. They did not, however, have the time and needed to share findings when they could be used to shape health programmes.

Many of the contexts where we work, whether these are in education, health-care, urban development, sanitation, etc. usually experience some sort of time and financial pressure. This means that if research is going to be used to inform decision-making in relation to new strategies, interventions or modifications to existing services, it needs to be delivered in a timely manner. As McNall and colleagues have argued for rapid evaluations, 'the timeliness of information is no less critical than its accuracy, as exigencies often force program managers to make decisions before thorough analyses can be completed' (2004: 287). Timeliness can mean developing rapid studies as well as designing longer studies with rapid feedback loops so findings can be shared at specific time points (i.e. before key meetings are to take place).

Another reason why we need rapid research is because long-term research might not be feasible. This is the case of researchers working in areas of conflict or in the context of complex health emergencies (Johnson and Vindrola-Padros 2017; Skaras 2018). In these cases, it might not be possible for researchers to carry out long-term fieldwork because it might put them at risk (Skaras 2018). They might also need to move quickly between communities or facilities to capture flows or shifting information that might not be available at a later date (such as in the case of researchers tracking the spread of epidemics) (Abramowitz et al. 2015).

Field research can also be expensive, and researchers might be working with limited budgets (Handwerker 2001). Different cost-cutting strategies might also need to be used during the analysis phase, with more focused analysis or selected transcription of interview recordings and observation notes (Johnson and Vindrola-Padros 2020). I have seen this occurring more frequently with doctoral students who are self-funding their fieldwork, and, therefore, have to become more 'research-efficient' and be strategic about how they cover their research expenses.

Another reason why rapid research might be used is that researchers might acknowledge the fact that long-term research is not necessary to obtain the data required to answer their research questions. Rapid research, if carried out properly, is capable of delivering high-quality studies. Some researchers have developed a series of strategies for guaranteeing the high quality of research and validity of the data despite the short study time frames. We will discuss these strategies across the book.

Vignette: The use of focused ethnographies in doctoral fieldwork

I teach an intensive course for doctoral students on rapid ethnographies. The course has a limit of attendees set at seventeen people. The first year I taught the course, about three to five people attended. The second year it was around eight people. Now, in its third year, the course is fully booked, with a waiting list. A reason for the increase in the number of attendees could be that it takes time for people to hear about these courses, and since it is an optional course, students need to hear from other students that the course is worth registering for. Another reason could be that students and supervisors are hearing about rapid research approaches and they are becoming more open to accepting these as a valid form of research design.

There is clearly a need for rapid or focused ethnographic approaches in many doctoral programmes. In the UK, doctoral programmes are normally three years long (with options for extending to a fourth year, in some cases). Many doctoral students in healthcare-related fields are encouraged to carry out a systematic literature review in their first year and will then focus on passing an upgrade examination, which moves them from MPhil to PhD candidate status. Many try to leave the last year for analysis and write-up, which means that, after factoring a study set-up period and ethical review, they have six to nine months for fieldwork. One of the main questions I receive from students taking my course is, 'I only have six months and need to make the most of it. Is this enough time?'

The trend described here mirrors other changes in ethnographic fieldwork during doctoral training discussed elsewhere (Faubion and Marcus 2009), yet, for the purpose of this book, it is important to highlight that the increase in the uptake of rapid or focused ethnographic research approaches by doctoral students and their supervisors can point to a potential radical expansion of the field of rapid ethnographies in forthcoming generations. It can also point to its reconfiguration, as many of these early career researchers are approaching rapid ethnographies with the passion and curiosity characteristic of many doctoral students. Their rapid ethnographies are many times independent projects, and although they must adhere to academic standards and departmental guidelines, they are often free to experiment more than those of us working in applied health fields who are accountable to external funders and clients. I see their work as an active test-bed of approaches and these students as the next leaders in this emerging field.

What Are the Challenges of Rapid Ethnographic Research?

A series of challenges for conducting studies of this sort have been identified in the literature (Vindrola-Padros and Vindrola-Padros 2018) (see Table 1.1). Researchers can face tensions between the breadth and depth of data, which might raise questions regarding the validity of data (Manderson and Aaby 1992a, 1992b). For instance, short-term fieldwork might not allow researchers to capture changes over time, understand all relevant sociocultural factors at stake or document conflicts and contradictions in findings (Bentley et al. 1988; Harris et al. 1997), thus potentially leading to unfounded interpretations and conclusions.

Rapid ethnographies often rely on the use of teams of field researchers (in contrast to the traditional lone-researcher model in ethnography) to collect greater volumes and wider diversity of data (Manderson and Aaby 1992b; Bentley et al. 1988). Team-based ethnographic research might influence the reliability of the data, as not all researchers will collect and analyse data in the same way. Shorter fieldwork periods also raise questions in relation to the representativeness of samples, as researchers may need to rely on the participants who are most accessible, losing diversity in experiences and points of view (Manderson and Aaby 1992b; Bentley et al. 1988; Harris et al. 1997; Utarini et al. 2001). Researchers might not have time to follow-up with participants to cross-check information or explore additional topics. Periods of data analysis might need to be compressed, affording little time for critical reflection (Utarini et al. 2001; Pink and Morgan 2013).

Another challenge for conducting rapid ethnographies is overcoming its representation as a 'quick and dirty' exercise with limited theoretical grounding and lack of critical analysis. In part, this association is the product of the history of rapid research, namely rapid assessment approaches, that tended to separate anthropological theory and method to produce instruments or tools for rapid fieldwork (Manderson and Aaby 1992b; Pink and Morgan 2013). Current debates, particularly in relation to rapid ethnographies, have highlighted that overreliance on the production of 'actionable findings' might make ethnographies too instrumental and lose sight of 'how well quality improvement endeavours are aligned with the cultural context and the interests of those working or receiving care in the setting' (Cupit et al. 2018). Some authors have also called into question the nature of the knowledge produced through rapid ethnographic research (Cupit et al. 2018; Manderson and Aaby 1992b). Furthermore, if rapid ethnographies are framed solely as research for improvement, ethnographers might have to limit the research to the elements of interest to the improvement teams, producing what other authors have referred to as 'ethnography lite',

Table 1.1 Main challenges of carrying out rapid ethnographies

Potential challenges	Description of the challenge	Key literature discussing challenge
'Breadth' versus 'depth' in data collection	Rapid study time frames might mean researchers do not have the capacity to capture changes over time, understand all relevant social and cultural factors at stake or identify conflicts and contradictions.	Manderson and Aaby 1992a, 1992b; Bentley et al. 1988; Pink and Morgan 2013
Representativeness and sample size and selection	Shorter fieldwork periods might mean that researchers will rely on those informants who are most accessible and lose the multiplicity of voices (and conflicting views).	Manderson and Aaby 1992a, 1992b; Bentley et al. 1988; Pink and Morgan 2013; Harris et al. 1997
Use and training of local research assistants	Local research assistants are not always available, have the required skills or willingness to take part. Training takes time, and research undertaken by researchers without an anthropological background might limit the quality of the study.	Manderson and Aaby 1992a, 1992b; Bentley et al. 1988; Harris et al. 1997
Lone researcher vs. research team	Teams with multiple researchers can maximize resources and cover a wide range of expertize. Recruitment might be an issue and clear roles in the field need to be outlined. Mechanisms need to be established to ensure consistency in data collection and analysis across all team members.	Manderson and Aaby 1992a; Bentley et al. 1988
'In and out' researcher vs. long-term engagement	Researchers that are new in the field might get additional attention but lack familiarity with the topic, context and local relationships. Prolonged engagement often increases credibility and internal validity. Prolonged engagement might also lead to stronger relationships between participants and researchers, potentially allowing researchers access to other types of information.	Manderson and Aaby 1992a, 1992b; Pink and Morgan 2013; Harris et al. 1997
Time for reflexivity	Rapid study time frames might limit the amount of critical reflection researchers are able to undergo during data collection and analysis. The writing time, style and format of the writing might limit researchers' ability to introduce a reflexive stance into the text.	Utarini et al. 2001; Harris et al. 1997
Research governance and ethical principles	Lengthy processes for ethical approval might limit researchers' capacity to enter the field quickly.	Pink and Morgan 2013; Harris et al. 1997

Source: Vindrola-Padros and Vindrola-Padros 2018.

diluted research without immersion and reflective practice (Singh 2005; Sobo 2012).

Authors have expressed concerns about the validity of rapid research and the need for frameworks to address the quality and rigour of rapid studies and evaluation (Nunns 2009; McNall and Foster-Fishman 2007). Recent reviews of rapid ethnographies and rapid qualitative research methods in health service delivery have highlighted the poor quality of reporting of study designs, lack of clarity regarding the defining characteristics of rapid research approaches, and missing information on how study findings are shared and used to make changes in practice (Johnson and Vindrola-Padros 2017; Vindrola-Padros and Vindrola-Padros 2018). The authors of these reviews have highlighted the need to develop a framework to define and describe methodologies rigorously, and outline how findings are used (Johnson and Vindrola-Padros 2017; Vindrola-Padros and Vindrola-Padros 2018).

Structure of the Book

The book will provide an overview of the main features of different types of rapid ethnographies, identifying challenges and modifications made when these have been carried out in practice. I use case studies of rapid ethnographies to illustrate the main concepts discussed in the chapter.

This introductory chapter sets out the aims of the book and its overall structure. The purpose of this chapter is to provide you with definitions and the characteristic features of rapid research. It proposes a threshold for distinguishing rapid research from long-term research, while also problematising distinctions based purely on the duration of the study. An important aspect of the chapter is to help you identify when rapid research is suitable and useful. The chapter also briefly explores the main challenges of carrying rapid research, such as maintaining a clear theoretical grounding of the research despite time pressures, dealing with the tension between the breadth and depth of data, addressing potential issues with sampling where recruitment might be limited to those who are most accessible, devoting limited time to reflexivity and addressing potential delays in the management and governance of the research. These challenges are explored in greater detail in the rest of the chapters.

Chapter 2 presents the key debates in the field of rapid ethnography and the assumptions associated with conventional ethnographic research. This chapter discusses the particular characteristics of rapid ethnographies. The chapter engages with discussions on epistemology, the role of theory and reflexivity in ethnographic research and the role these occupy in rapid ethnographies. These have been limitations identified by proponents of focused ethnographies (Knoblauch 2005) and short-term ethnographies (Pink and Morgan 2013), so this chapter seeks to provide evidence of how rapid ethnographies can also engage with theory and the reflective practice that characterises more 'traditional' forms of ethnography.

Chapter 3 presents an overview of work carried out prior to the emergence of rapid ethnographies. It briefly goes over approaches such as rapid rural appraisals (RRA), participatory rural appraisals (PRA), rapid ethnographic assessments (REA), rapid assessment procedures (RAP), rapid assessment response and evaluation (RARE), rapid appraisals, rapid qualitative inquiry (RQI) and rapid evaluation. The purpose of the chapter is to situate rapid ethnographies within a wider field of rapid research, demonstrating the diversity of approaches and their rich history. The chapter also makes comparisons across rapid approaches to highlight their characteristic features and trends that have developed in the way in which we do rapid research.

Chapter 4 is based on more recent rapid ethnographic approaches for lone researchers: quick ethnographies proposed by Handwerker (2001), focused ethnographies proposed by Knoblauch (2005) and short-term ethnographies proposed by Pink and Morgan (2013). A step-by-step guide for designing and implementing these types of ethnographies is included, as well as a discussion of the benefits and limitations of using these approaches. This chapter also includes three case studies, one for each type of rapid ethnography and a description of a rapid ethnography I carried out.

Chapter 5 follows a similar process, but for team-based ethnographies. In this chapter, I introduce you to team-based focused ethnographies, rapid site-switching ethnographies and a specific approach developed for ethnographic research in the context of clinical trials called RAPICE (Palinkas and Zatzick 2019). I present step-by-step guides for the design and implementation of these approaches and discuss the particular challenges of carrying out rapid ethnographies as a team. I also describe a rapid ethnography our team carried out recently.

Chapter 6 covers issues related to ethics and the main challenges of this type of research. A series of challenges have been identified in rapid ethnographies, which are mainly produced by time pressures, the reliance on teams of field researchers, the instrumental or pragmatic nature of some rapid designs (which might jeopardise the independence of the research) and the lack of attention paid to theory and reflexivity. As a consequence, rapid ethnographies are often thought of being 'quick and dirty'. It includes a discussion of ethical governance processes, arguing that even though studies must be carried out quickly, the same ethical principles as those of long-term studies must be followed (i.e. informed consent, do no harm, confidentiality and anonymity). It presents a few strategies for streamlining the review of applications for ethical approval, showing examples of ethical review committees around the world that have established quicker and simpler review processes for studies that are low risk and time-sensitive. The chapter reviews a series of rapid tools and techniques currently used in qualitative research to reduce the amount of time required for data collection and analysis. These tools and techniques include bypassing the use of transcripts by analysing directly from interview recordings, using selected transcription or speeding up the development of transcripts through on-site scribes or voice-recognition software. The chapter also includes a brief description of the emotional labour involved in rapid ethnographic research.

Many of the rapid ethnographic approaches presented in this book were developed to produce 'actionable findings', that is, findings that can be used to make changes in policy and/or practice. However, there is limited knowledge of how findings are normally disseminated in rapid ethnographies, and, even less, on how these findings are used. Chapter 7 outlines the strategies that can be used throughout all stages of the research to maximise its impact. It highlights the importance of developing groups of stakeholders who can act in an advisory capacity throughout the study, ensuring the study is relevant, but also facilitating the incorporation of findings into changes in practice. The chapter also proposes the establishment of regular feedback loops, where findings from the study are shared on a continuous basis and not only after the study has ended. The frequency and format of feedback is also discussed, and the chapter proposes different alternatives for disseminating information (i.e. written reports, infographics, videos, podcasts, etc.).

Even though rapid methods are not new, two recent reviews on the use of rapid qualitative methods in healthcare have shown a recent increase in their popularity (Johnson and Vindrola-Padros 2017; Vindrola-Padros and Vindrola-Padros 2018). One of the main findings of both reviews, however, was the prevalence of gaps in the reporting of the study design and process of implementation. The authors called for the development of guidelines or a reporting framework to ensure rapid research has a robust design and is reported in detail in publications. One of the topics of Chapter 8 is future plans to develop these standards. The chapter also explores recent developments in methodological innovation that have resulted in new 'spin-offs' of rapid ethnographies and a proposal for the development of training programmes on the topic. The chapter ends with an agenda for the future development of the field of rapid ethnography.

The book is sprinkled with vignettes from my own experience of carrying out field-based research in five countries over many years and case studies, which are examples published by other authors. It also contains several resources in the form of appendices. I include tools used for data collection in rapid ethnographies that might be helpful for those designing studies. I have also developed an annotated bibliography of quick, rapid, focused and short-term ethnographies I have identified to date. When I was just starting out in the field of rapid research, I found reviewing rapid ethnographies and mapping their study designs a really useful exercise. Another resource in the appendices is a list of suggested reading material (some of which is not cited in the book). When I teach on this topic, I often give my students printed copies of this list so they can make notes on it as we go through the content. In the case of this book, the purpose of the list is to point you to literature that will help you gain deeper insight into specific topics. The book was designed as an introductory resource, so I have discussed some topics in superficial form. This list, as well as our lab's website (www.ucl.ac .uk/qualitative-health-research-network/rreal-rapid-research-evaluation-and-appraisal-lab), can be useful resources for obtaining more in-depth and up-to-date information. Other resources in the appendices are sign-posted throughout the book.

Using the Book Content

The book is designed so its contents can be used in different ways. One way is go through the chapters in their current order: general introduction, theoretical discussion, historical overview, description of general types of study designs and implementation approaches, discussion of practicalities and ethical dilemmas, overview of dissemination strategies, and future of the field. Another way is to select specific chapters that might be the only ones relevant for your work (the chapters are written as standalone pieces, even though they might cross-refer to content in other chapters).

If used as a teaching tool, I have often used the content of the book to guide students through the stages of designing and implementing their own rapid ethnographies. After finishing each chapter, they are tasked with integrating the main concepts and suggestions discussed in the chapter into their own studies. This entails, for instance, using Chapter 1 to consider if their topic is suitable for a rapid design, reflecting on the potential opportunities and limitations of using rapid ethnographies for this particular study (based on Chapter 2), taking into consideration other rapid approaches such as the ones presented in Chapter 3, identifying methods for data collection and analysis for their own study (Chapters 4 and 5), addressing the practical considerations outlined in Chapter 6 and developing their own dissemination plan (Chapter 7).

Vignette: My first rapid ethnography attempt

Thinking back, I think my first exposure to rapid ethnography was when I was carrying out fieldwork for my doctoral dissertation. I was studying at a university in the US but wanted to carry out the fieldwork in Argentina. I was interested in exploring processes of internal medical travel in cases of children diagnosed with cancer. Argentina has a centralised medical system, where hospitals with specialist services for cancer treatment are mainly located in the capital. This meant families needed to travel from different areas of the country to access care, remaining several months away from home and other members of the family. Accompanying parents often lost their jobs and children had to interrupt their education. Many families also struggled to cover the costs of travel and relocation.

Part of my funding during doctoral training depended on work I carried out during term-time as a research assistant for the Department of Anthropology and as an instructor for a few courses on the Anthropology Bachelor's programme. This meant that I would need to find alternative sources of funding to be able to travel to Argentina to carry out fieldwork for an extended period of time. Despite applying for multiple doctoral fieldwork fellowships and grants, I was not successful and needed to keep my roles as research assistant and instructor in the department to cover my living expenses. I would only have three summer terms (during which I did not have any income) to travel to Argentina to collect data.

This meant that, in many ways, I would need to consider a rapid ethnography design out of the need to pursue a study that I was deeply passionate about but where I did not have funding to sustain long-term fieldwork. I would need to be strategic throughout the year to save enough money to live for three months without income over the summer and cover travel expenses to and from Buenos Aires. I also needed to demonstrate to an Anthropology Department, where students normally engaged in twelve to eighteen months of continuous fieldwork, that my research design of carrying out three short periods of fieldwork would be equally valid.

As I designed the study, the benefits of engaging in multiple short-term field visits became even clearer. Many of the families I would be working with would remain in Buenos Aires for a few weeks or months, would go back to their place of origin for a few weeks months and come back. This is how the treatment plan was designed, and they would be allowed to go home for periods when they were not receiving treatment, if there were no complication and the child did not have any signs of immunosuppression. The detailed tracking of patients' journeys that formed part of my study design could alert me to the months when families would be making their way back to Buenos Aires and I could arrange to meet them again and continue with data collection.

I was then able to organise data collection in three periods of intensive fieldwork (each lasting three months), following families through their internal journeys in Buenos Aires, while they visited the hospitals, their temporary housing, pharmacies, the Oncology Drug Bank and a wide range of government institutions where they requested support for travel, unemployment and medical expenses. Each visit also allowed me to capture changes in hospital services and government policies through time. By spreading out my visits, I was able to document changes over a four-year period.

Conclusion

In this chapter, I shared a personal experience of proposing rapid and collaborative ethnographic research designs to colleagues with the goal of pointing to the tensions prevalent in the relationship between rapid and conventional ethnography. I have explored the importance of timeliness in research and how rapid research approaches, such as rapid ethnographies, have been developed to address this need. Methodological experimentation does not come without challenges, so I have spent a considerable portion of the chapter going over these and some strategies researchers have used to address them. I have laid out the structure of the book to guide you on the best way to use the content and the resources found in the appendices. The layout of the book as well as these resources were developed after I asked myself what I would have found helpful when I was starting out in this field. I hope you feel you can roam freely throughout the book, teasing out the content relevant for you, unpacking and dissecting chapters, and applying the learning to your own work.

2 | Key Debates in the Field of Rapid Ethnographies

> Something called 'ethnography' is perpetually undone and redone, and as a result, fetishized, protected, or freely reinvented. Ethnographic 'value' is thus forever in the process of being translated, reconstituted, recirculated.
>
> (Reddy 2009: 108)

As I highlighted in the opening story in the introduction chapter, the development of rapid ethnographies has not gone uncontested in the social sciences. A lot of this resistance has emerged as a result of different conceptualisations of the role of research in society (the 'pure' vs. 'applied' debate) and the responsibility of the ethnographer towards those communities and individuals who share their time and stories with them. I would also argue that a lot of this resistance is due to misconceptions about what rapid ethnographies are and what they are trying to achieve. In this chapter, I have outlined the key assumptions about conventional and rapid ethnography to dispel the 'myths' and misconceptions of rapid ethnographic research. I also use the discussions to critically analyse the design and implementation of rapid ethnographies to date and highlight the limitations of these approaches.

Assumptions about Conventional and Rapid Ethnographies

Debates in relation to the mainstream use of rapid ethnography have extended beyond anthropology and have taken many forms. In this section, I have tried to summarise the underlying assumptions guiding these discussions. Most of these debates have centred on the validity of rapid ethnography as a research approach, the credibility of the ethnographer using rapid ethnography, and the potential negative consequences the mainstream use of rapid ethnography can have on conventional ethnography and the production of knowledge in general.

The main debate is based on defining the 'appropriate' amount of time required for fieldwork in ethnographic research. Even though there are no universally set standards for this length of time (some say one year, others two, others refer to life-time engagement), many anthropologists argue that ethnographic research takes time. Some have even stated that long-term fieldwork is part of the definition of ethnography, and therefore, shorter studies cannot be classified as 'genuine ethnography' (Wolcott 1980). This idea of a minimum amount of time required in the field is associated with five main assumptions:

1. Ethnographers need time to generate relationships with key informants and other participants, and as these relationships develop, ethnographers obtain greater insight into the lives of their participants and their own predispositions.
2. Ethnographers need to spend an extended amount of time in the field to capture changes in relation to topics that are of interest to the research questions guiding the study (for instance, understanding how these vary based on the different seasons in the year).
3. The longer the ethnographer does fieldwork, the better they are able to capture the richness and complexity of everyday life.
4. An extended amount of time in the field allows the ethnographer to capture events or situations that were not originally anticipated (the serendipitous quality of ethnographic research).
5. The crafting of the ethnographic text takes time; it is an iterative process that cannot be rushed.
6. Short-term ethnographic research is not able to engage in key processes for the production of knowledge prevalent in conventional ethnography, which entail reflection on one's own positionality.

Ethnographers Require Time to Generate Relationships

Without underestimating the value of long-term fieldwork (I myself have been studying medical travel for pediatric oncology treatment in Argentina for over ten years), I think all of the assumptions listed above can be queried. The first assumption is based on the premise that extended presence in an area can lead to the development of relationships. The interaction with participants in an informal and open way can obviously lead to the development of relationships, but this is not only a matter of time; it is based on the predisposition of the ethnographer to create these relationships in the first place. My experience is that researchers doing rapid ethnographies can create meaningful relationships in the field (meaningful being defined in relation to the purpose of the study and its research questions). Furthermore, some rapid ethnographies entail multiple short fieldwork visits to the same location, where ethnographers are able to reconnect with contacts. In many cases, fieldwork is not carried out in a distant and detached location from where the ethnographer lives, so even though data might not be actively collected, ethnographers are able to see these key informants in a different capacity, further developing these relationships. These fieldwork arrangements call into question bounded notions of the field, where one enters or leaves at particular times, and instead point towards a field that is constructed and performed (not there to be discovered), partial and negotiated, and even integrated into the daily lives of ethnographers once they have finished fieldwork (Amit 2000; Coleman and Collins 2006). It might be as Appadurai (1988) argued, where in an interconnected world we never actually leave the field.

In a text I have titled, *Looking at the Field from Afar and Bringing It Closer to Home*, I reflect on the permeability of the field in the cases of anthropologists who do research where they live and who might even receive services or care at their fieldsites (Vindrola-Padros 2019). I explore personal experiences of giving birth and remaining hospitalised with my newborn baby in the health system that has been one of my fieldsites for eight years. I ask: Where does the field start and where does it end? Have I stopped building relationships because I am no longer collecting data? Have I stopped understanding my field because I am not physically there?

Faubion's (2009) appeal to reconceptualise fieldwork might be helpful here. According to this author, we need to consider fieldwork beyond the data collection carried out at the fieldsite and consider all other encounters that allow us to make sense of what we have encountered in the field (Faubion 2009). He refers to time passed at the library, or conversations with students and colleagues that contribute to this meaning-making process (Faubion 2009). To this I would like to add that we also consider relationship-building in a different way, as many ethnographers continue to be in communication with key informants through e-mail, phone calls and, now more frequently, social media. Relationship-building with key informants is a process that moves beyond the time the ethnographer physically spends at the fieldsite.

At one of the sites where we have carried out a rapid ethnography of a nursing intervention, we have a WhatsApp group that brings together many of the key people I worked with throughout the study. Through this group, I received updates on the service, even months after our formal data collection ended. We also used the group to share news about what was happening in the country, our families and how we were feeling at particular times. Happy birthday messages, with cake emoji, were also common.

Ethnographic Fieldwork Needs to Be Long to Capture Changes over Time

When discussing the historical background to the establishment of the 'appropriate' amount of time anthropology doctoral students need to spend in the field, Jeffrey and Troman (2004) argue that the initial time frame of two years in the field was related to the agricultural calendar and established so students could observe their communities under the different seasons (i.e. wet and dry) and the cultural and social activities associated with these. These authors argue that this fieldwork model might be less relevant for the type of ethnographies that are carried out now, where changes in the field might be associated with other temporalities (Jeffrey and Troman 2004).

When teaching about rapid ethnographies, I often get approached by students who are interested in carrying out research on topics that I find are more amenable to long-term ethnographic research. These topics normally entail tracking a service or the implementation of a programme over time. The first thing we do is see if we can capture these changes through a rapid design where the student can carry out multiple intensive site visits over time and comparing changes in the service or programme across the different site visits. If we feel relevant data will be missed during the periods of time the student will not be in the field, then we discard the idea of a rapid design and work on the premise that the study will require long-term fieldwork.

It is important to note that several rapid ethnographies have been successful in examining changes over time using a series of intensive site visits. Some of these have also been multi-sited ethnographies, so they have captured changes across time and space. For instance, McKeown et al. (2020) carried out a rapid ethnography across fourteen acute mental health Trusts in the UK, dividing the fieldwork in two one-week intensive fieldwork intervals, before and after the implementation of an intervention aimed at reducing the use of physical restraint for mental health patients. This type of design allowed the research team to identify the elements in organisational culture and practice that had changed as a result of the implementation of the intervention and those that remained the same (McKeown et al. 2020).

Ethnographic Research Needs to Be Long to Capture Complex Social Processes

A key assumption in the long-term/rapid ethnography debate is based on the premise that the ethnographer will not be able to document and understand complex social processes in a short amount of time. In a recent special issue on ethnography and evaluation, Reynolds and Lewis (2019) unpack the association of ethnographic research with the analysis of complexity in health evaluation research. In this context, complexity is understood as the ability to uncover and take into consideration the multiple mechanisms and interactions between the intervention that is being implemented, the context/s where it is implemented and the actors involved in the process. It would seek to capture all of the actions involved in implementation and apply anthropology's holistic lens to analyse how these actions are shaped by the wider healthcare system (Reynolds and Lewis 2019).

Time spent in the field, however, does not necessarily guarantee being able to capture this complexity (or to make sense of it). I am sure most of us can probably reference long-term research that has not been able to reach this goal. Lewis and Russell argue that ethnography does not depend on the amount of time spent in the field, but on the ethnographer's attitude towards 'being there' (2011: 400). I would argue that it is this attitude that allows ethnographers to capture complexity, not the amount of time spent in the field. In the words of Wolcott (1980; 56), 'one could do a participant-observer study from now to doomsday and never come up with a sliver of ethnography. [. . .] We are fast losing sight of the fact that the essential ethnographic contribution is interpretive rather than methodological.' The ethnographic interpretive frame is the main reason why ethnographic research is able to capture and make sense of complex social processes, whether the researcher spends six months in the field or two years.

Ethnography, Time and Serendipity

Several anthropologists have argued that one of the defining characteristics of ethnographic research is its conceptual openness, in the sense that ethnographers allow themselves to be surprised by the events and situations they find in the field (Lewis et al. 2018; Rivoal and Salazar 2013). They refer to the serendipitous nature of many discoveries made in the field, situations that had not been planned or anticipated by ethnographers, which allowed them to open entirely new areas of inquiry. Some anthropologists have argued that in order to allow for serendipity, ethnographers need to spend a considerable amount of time in the field (Rivoal and Salazar 2013). Rivoal and Salazar argue, for instance, that 'serendipitous research requires time-making time to observe, understand and ponder, and stretching time, if needed, to go back and forth between the traditionally separated periods of data gathering and analysis' (2013: 3). 'Being there' requires active field research as well as 'spaces between action' (Palmer et al. 2017), where ethnographers wait for these unanticipated events to arrive and allow for the emergence of new knowledge (Lewis et al. 2018; Mannay and Morgan 2015). Ethnography also requires this back and forth between collecting and making sense of data.

Similarly to the assumptions discussed so far, my argument would be that serendipity is not dependent on the time spent in the field, but on the predisposition of the ethnographer. Serendipity emerges in ethnography, not because the researcher is in the field for a long time, but due to a disciplinary inclination where sociocultural processes can be studied without needing to decide in advance on the ontology or scale of these processes (Dalakoglou and Harvey 2012). It is this resistance to deciding in advance and remaining open to what is encountered in the field, even if it goes against the initial beliefs or assumptions of the ethnographer, even if it makes the ethnographer uncomfortable, that makes a study ethnographic. Rivoal and Salazar (2013) argue that the field shapes the research and the ethnographer to some extent; I would argue that this is true for both short-term and long-term research, and it depends on the ethnographer's willingness to be shaped.

The Creation of the Ethnographic Text

The analysis of the creation of the ethnographic text in anthropology is intertwined with discussions around authority and its negotiation. According to Geertz (1988), this authority is created in the flow between 'being there' (during fieldwork) and the 'here' (where the text is written). By 'being there' the anthropologist becomes a witness to the social realities at stake and, in the text, must persuade the reader that this process of 'being there' gives them the authority to speak for others (Bond 1990; Clifford 1983; Rabinow 1986). The literary turn in the social sciences called into question this notion of authority, proposing a more relational, partial and negotiated concept (Jackson 2016; Punch 2012). It also pointed to the incompleteness of the text and power relations involved in its creation (Abu-Lughod 1991).

'Being there', however, has remained one of the central markers of anthropological value and credibility. As Gupta and Ferguson (1997: 1) have argued, 'the single most significant factor determining whether a piece of research will be accepted as (that magical word) "anthropological" is the extent to which it depends on experience in the field".' There is a connection between this experience in the field and what the ethnographer is able to describe authoritatively in the ethnographic text. Rapid ethnographies are often critiqued because the amount of time spent in the field is not considered enough to give the ethnographer the credibility to write authoritatively in the text. As Amit (2000) has argued, duration of fieldwork and its long-term and thorough immersion make fieldwork anthropological. In addition, many ethnographers developing rapid or focused ethnographies do not have enough time to produce the rich ethnographic texts that characterise conventional ethnography.

The term 'ethnography' is mainly used in anthropology to refer to the text that is produced as a result of fieldwork. According to Van Maanen (2011), ethnographies sit between the cultural world of those who share their stories with us and the world of the ethnographer and readers. In many ways, the creation of the ethnographic text is the product of interpretive processes that translate one world into a language intelligible to the second one. This process of translation is iterative and implies a high degree of emotional labour. Many argue that it is a process that takes time and cannot be rushed. When we carried out our review of rapid ethnographies in healthcare (Vindrola-Padros and Vindrola-Padros 2018), we were interested in exploring the extent to which authors tried to maintain a sense of the ethnographic narrative in their articles. We have only found one rapid ethnography written in the form of a book; the rest were articles or remained in the grey literature in the form of reports. Even those published as articles tended to replicate styles of writing that aligned themselves more with articles published in nursing or medicine, and had little resemblance to more anthropological articles. Some authors have highlighted this finding as a concern, as it leads to creations of a text that might lose the artistic dimensions of the conventional ethnographic text and, instead, become dry and instrumental (in the sense that it only shares the findings required to inform decision-making, and does so under the restrictions of a 5,000-word limit) (Cupit et al. 2018).

The question for us is more profound: Will rapid ethnographies, within their compressed time frames, be able to capture the same level of interpretation, or 'thick description', as conventional ethnographies? One answer, 'no, they will not' is easy. A second type of answer could be 'yes and no, as they might capture richness, but in a different way or format'. A third, more controversial, answer could be 'yes, and they can actually do more collaborative interpretive work'. The first answer will probably be given by someone who will not be supportive of the use of rapid ethnographies because they will never be able to reach the level of interpretive work reached by conventional ethnographies. There is not much work we can do there. The two other points of view, however, recognise the value of rapid ethnographies as an approach distinct to conventional ethnographies.

In 2013, Pink and Morgan wrote a seminal piece on the use of short-term ethnographies, where they sought to set out an approach that had "different methodological, practical and analytical entry points into the lives of others" (Pink and Morgan 2013). According to these authors, if short-term ethnographies were to be embraced by the academic community, we would need to move beyond seeing short study time frames as limitations and, instead, recognise that intensive fieldwork and a different delineation of 'the field' could still produce valuable and reliable ways of knowing (Pink and Morgan 2013). Drawing from Pink's (2006, 2014, 2015) expertise in visual anthropology, the authors proposed the use of visual methods to both capture and represent the richness of the ethnographic encounter. Their answer to our question would probably be that it can be done, but the format might need to be different to allow for more intensive forms of fieldwork, interpretation and representation.

Another way to think about this question could be to think about rapid ethnographies as a way to transform conventional ethnography, including the creation of the ethnographic text. Let's go back to the brief description of my participation in the ethnography and cancer conference that I included in the introduction. Not only did the audience oppose the concept of a rapid ethnography; they also opposed the idea that it could be collaborative. The idea of collaborative ethnography is not new, and there is plenty of literature out there describing its benefits (Lassiter 2005, 2008). My proposal might have created immediate opposition because it touched on notions of authority and disciplinary identity as the ones I have described at the beginning of this section. My experience with rapid ethnography is that, by design, it depends a lot more on the development of collaborative relationship with those who share their stories with us. Many rapid ethnographies could not be carried out without these ties. Its iterative design also demands the collection and analysis of data in parallel, to share emerging findings with key stakeholders (often strengthening relationships), but also to cross-check interpretations with those in the field (as the ethnographer will not be able to do this at a later date).

You might expect that these relationships and iterative analysis have the potential to generate rich and textured descriptions of the social processes under study, whether these are in a text or not. Furthermore, Anthropology has, to some extent, already questioned the primacy of the text as a form of representation (Coffey 1996; Warren 2000). Another question for future rapid ethnographies is whether they will be able to generate alternative forms of representation that maintain ethnography's commitment to complexity, critical reflection and theoretical engagement. It might be too early to determine if this possible, but this could be an exciting aim for future work.

Time and the Critical Analysis of the Production of Knowledge

One of the key qualities of ethnographic research is its critical reflection of the processes used to produce knowledge, including an analysis of how the ethnographer shapes them. As we have argued elsewhere, 'one of the central components of ethnographic research is the researcher's critical account of their "self-location" (gender, class, ethnicity, and so on), interests, preassumptions and life experiences and how these shape their relationships with study participants and the research process itself' (Vindrola-Padros and Vindrola-Padros 2018: 7). Unfortunately, our review of rapid ethnographies in healthcare found little evidence of critical reflection on the ethnographer's positionality, and we identified this as a serious limitation in the development of this field of work. Other authors have highlighted this limitation, pointing to the instrumentality of rapid ethnographies (Cupit et al. 2018), the domination of positivist frameworks and their failure to engage with the politics of knowledge production (Vougioukalou et al. 2019).

The main concern is that time pressures might reduce ethnography to method, that is, to the reporting of data obtained through interviews and observations, without critical engagement with social theory (Vougioukalou et al. 2019; Waring and Jones 2016). I would argue that this lack of theoretical engagement does not need to be a consequence of the widespread use of rapid ethnographies. Engagement with social theory, and the implementation of a critical lens, has actually been a defining characteristic of some rapid ethnographies such as short-term ethnography (Pink and Morgan 2013), quick ethnography (Handwerker 2001) and focused ethnography (Knoblauch 2005). It all depends on how the rapid ethnography is carried out, the long-standing distinction Beebe (2004) asked us to make between 'rapid' and 'rushed' research.

This doesn't mean that we can't make improvements in the design and implementation of rapid ethnographies. In a recent publication where we outlined six proposed characteristics of rapid ethnographies, we added one characteristic which reads, 'the research engages with anthropological and other social science theories and promotes reflexivity' (Vindrola-Padros and Vindrola-Padros 2018) to motivate future rapid ethnographies to have theory at the core of the research. Some recent publications of rapid ethnographies have already engaged successfully with this call (see Vougioukalou et al. 2019).

'Purists' vs. 'Pragmatists' and Ethnography as a Changing Practice

In a recent article, Vougioukalou et al. (2019) argue that current debates on the use of ethnographic research for quality improvement can be understood by grouping authors as either purists or pragmatists. The purists value what 'ought to be done', while the pragmatists value what 'can be done' (Vougioukalou et al. 2019). For instance, authors such as Waring and Jones (2016) have focused their discussion on what constitutes 'proper ethnography', that is, identifying the level of organisational study design that can be considered ethnographic and advocating for research that does not comply with this level to avoid references to ethnography (Vougioukalou et al. 2019). Their arguments resonate with other pieces of work in anthropology that have, rather nostalgically, warned against the dangers of recent appropriations of the 'ethnography label', where rapid ethnographies are seen as instrumental, diluted, 'airplane ethnographies' or 'ethnography lite' (Cupit et al. 2018; Jowsey 2016; Bate 1997). In contrast, many of the researchers using rapid or focused ethnographic approaches have argued that these approaches can preserve ethnographic qualities in shorter study time frames, narrower enquiries and more intensive forms of fieldwork (Vougioukalou et al. 2019; Pink and Morgan 2013).

I would argue that there is a third point of view in this debate (one that I align myself with), which is based on the idea that the production of knowledge through ethnographic research responds to the changing nature of the social realities we study, so, consequently, it will always be under some form of transformation. In their attempt to preserve 'appropriate forms of ethnographic research', the 'purists' have overlooked the fact that there are a wide range of ways to carry out ethnographic research and these are constantly changing. This has led to a certain degree of defensiveness in relation to the use of ethnography label, one that is artificial as nothing seems to be under attack (as I asked in the introduction of this book, what were they defending?).

In 1995, when Marcus first made the case to carry out multi-sited ethnographies, he was questioning place-based concepts of culture and traditional models of single-sited research that had prevailed in ethnographic imaginaries up until this time (even if ethnographic research had always been, to some extent, multi-sited) (Coleman and Collins 2006). His proposal for a multi-sited ethnography went beyond solely considering the dynamic relationships between the local and the global and the need to understand factors operating at the system level and how these were reconfigured in everyday practice (Coleman and von Hellermann 2006; Marcus 1995, 2006). Marcus was actually proposing a more dramatic reconfiguration of how we visualised and performed ethnographic research, by moving beyond the ethnographer–other binary to more collective ways of thinking about and doing ethnography (Marcus 2006).

Sarah Pink's (2006, 2014, 2015) work on visual and sensory ethnography called into question the primacy of the ethnographic text as a way of making sense of ethnographic data and representing those we study. Pink has urged us to rethink ethnography through the senses and explore new ways of using sensory arts practice to engage with the communities where we work (Pink 2015). Anthropologists have proposed new fields and ways of doing field research appropriate to these, including the use of virtual ethnography or netography to explore social relationships and interactions on online platforms (Hine 2015; Kozinets 2010), the integration of experimental co-design practices such as scenic design practices into ethnographic research production (Hegel et al. 2019), the (re)presentation of ethnographic data in theatrical performances (Madison 2018) and the shifting of the ethnographic lens to the self (instead of others) in auto-ethnographies (Sinden-Carroll 2018), to name a few. My argument is that rapid and focused ethnographies could represent one of the latest forms of transformation of ethnographic practice by experimenting with the time required to produce knowledge.

Ethnographic research is currently being used in a wide range of fields, each with its own requirements, opportunities and pace. It can make important contributions to the way in which we deliver services and other forms of care (as described in the vignette below). Shouldn't we be moving towards a more in-depth exploration of how we can make ethnography relevant for the main problems affecting our society today?

Vignette: The value of an ethnographic lens in applied health research

When I began working in a hospital in the UK a few years ago, some managers were trying to implement a new system for scheduling doctor consultations that used a fixed template for assigning appointments. At that time, waiting times for certain outpatient services were long, causing patient dissatisfaction and delays in the delivery of care. Each service organised their own appointments using simple tools such as spreadsheets and, in some cases, paper-based recording. This meant errors were frequent and information was sometimes lost.

The new system would ensure all services used the same online template. The template had fixed time slots with some flexibility for overbooking at the beginning and end of the day. After several months of development, the new system was piloted among a small group of services. Doctors from these services were asked to join a meeting where the new system would be launched.

The presentation of the new system was not well received by most doctors, as concerns were voiced regarding the suitability of the system for some services. Doctors were not happy they were not consulted when the new system was designed, thus disregarding their opinions and needs. A decision was made to continue piloting the system regardless of these concerns. Most doctors resisted the roll-out of the new system and continued to use their own spreadsheets and paper-based booking methods.

Some of the staff in charge of the new system told me that the reason why the system was not working was because 'the doctors' culture makes them resistant to change.' Management viewed the new system as part of a 'culture change' where doctors needed to align to a new standard way of working. Their 'culture' was seen as homogeneous, easily identifiable and static (with no inclination to change).

The conversations I had with doctors painted a different picture. First, not all doctors thought the new system was a bad idea; some liked it and felt it would help them organise their services better. However, they did not engage with the new system because they felt the hospital would eventually discontinue its use. Other doctors who liked the system were not able to voice their approval because they were in junior positions or had recently transferred from another hospital, and since several senior doctors in the service opposed the new system, they felt they also needed to be seen against it.

For doctors who did not like the new system, the main reason was that it was not designed in relation to the requirements of their service. Doctors wanted to be able to shape the appointments in relation to their patients' needs and combine outpatient consultations with private practice, inpatient rounds or academic commitments. Some also felt that the fixed time-slot booking method did not reflect the amount of time some patients required during consultation. In other words, the new system was not fit for purpose, as it did not reflect the needs of patients or the realities of care delivery in this setting.

Further discussions with the doctors highlighted that the hospital was entering harsh financial times, and many doctors did not agree with measures being put in place to reduce expenses. The new booking system was seen as one more of these measures, and for many of the doctors it was 'the final straw' of a working situation they were no longer willing to tolerate.

The situation described above demonstrates that the view held by management staff that 'the doctors' culture makes them resistant to change' did not account for the complex factors shaping the doctors' attitude towards the new system. It did not recognise that doctors are a heterogeneous group with different needs, patient-types, interests and capacity to influence other doctors. A focus on this heterogeneity would have allowed management staff the opportunity of identifying and working with the doctors who actually liked the new system. Furthermore, it would have allowed them to see that several doctors had already recognised that waiting time was a problem and had started to make changes in their own booking systems to deal with it. In a way, change was already happening. Had management staff consulted with doctors prior to implementing the new system, they may have also recognised that doctors are a multicultural group, bringing with them ways of working from other places, which can be adapted to suit the needs of their current hospital.

Doctors' perceptions of new initiatives do not operate in isolation from their local contexts, and other processes happening at the hospital level (e.g. budget cuts) can significantly influence their willingness to engage with new measures. Additionally, the way new initiatives are implemented from the top down might mean that doctors oppose them not for what they are but for the way in which they have been designed and communicated (or 'imposed' as some doctors argued).

In summary, an ethnographic study of doctors' daily practices indicated that their willingness to engage with a new way of working was influenced by the (un)suitability of the new system, power relations and hierarchies acting across the organisation, and the wider context of healthcare delivery. I shared these ideas with management staff while I worked at this hospital. While this perspective was incorporated in the development of other initiatives, much work needs to be done to ensure it becomes an integral part of their routine practice.

This case study was first discussed in Vindrola-Padros (2016).

Conclusion

The emergence of rapid ethnographies as a valid form of knowledge production has been contested in anthropology and other fields. In this chapter, I have argued that a lot of this debate is fuelled by assumptions regarding what conventional ethnography is (or should be) and pre-assumptions regarding the defining characteristics of rapid ethnographies. I have presented my view in relation to these assumptions based on the evidence found in the literature and years of experience in the field. I think that the takeaway message is that the limitations of rapid ethnographies have less to do with time and more to do with how these studies are implemented in practice. This is why the following chapters are dedicated to an exploration of the rich history of rapid research and the ways in which rapid ethnographies have been carried out to date.

3 | A Brief History of the Work Prior to Rapid Ethnographies

Anthropologists have been engaging with rapid ethnographic approaches since at least the 1970s. Some authors even mention examples around the 1950s when techniques such as *sondeo*, a quick survey or mapping of a particular area, were introduced (Hildebrand 1979; Beebe 2001). A wide range of rapid research approaches have been associated with ethnographic research, including rapid ethnographic assessments (REAs), rapid assessment procedures (RAPs), rapid assessment, response and evaluation (RARE), rapid appraisals, rapid assessment process and rapid qualitative inquiry (RQI). My perception is that they are influenced to some degree by ethnographic research and act as precursors to the rapid ethnographies described later in the book (see Table 3.1). I explore some of these in a different volume (Vindrola-Padros in preparation). For the purpose of this book, I refer to them in this chapter to make you aware that there are other forms of carrying out rapid research, and to highlight the rich history of rapid ethnographies.

The desire to shorten study time frames was based on several reasons. Perhaps the most salient one was the desire to use findings from ethnographic research to inform some type of programme planning, implementation or policy design (Scrimshaw and Hurtado 1987). Anthropologists acknowledged that if they wanted the findings of their studies to be used by others, they would need to adapt their study time frames to those of decision-makers. In a way, this meant that, even from its initial development, rapid ethnographies were inclined to be utilisation-focused research. Following Patton's (2002) definition of utilisation-focused evaluation, utilisation-focused research refers to research that is designed keeping in mind the ways in which the findings will be used. It involves the generation of knowledge with a purpose. This means that, to some extent, the history of rapid ethnographies has been shaped by shifts between academic and applied research.

Rapid Rural Appraisal (RRA)

Heywood (1990) defined rapid rural appraisals as 'a strategy for appraising a particular situation in the most cost-effective manner possible with appropriate levels of timeliness, accuracy and relevance'. RRAs depended on multidisciplinary teams, the combination of different sources of data and

Table 3.1 Rapid research approaches informed by ethnographic research

Approach	Brief definition	Key literature
Rapid rural appraisal (RRA)	'A strategy for appraising a particular situation in the most cost-effective manner possible with appropriate levels of timeliness, accuracy and relevance' (Heywood 1990).	Chambers 1980, 1992
Participatory rural appraisal (PRA)	'Methods were often highly flexible and qualitative in nature, employed multiple methods and triangulation, and adopted an approach which emphasized the importance of learning with, as well as from, local people' (Fitch et al. 2000).	Chambers 1994
Rapid ethnographic assessment (REA)	'A methodological approach that is intended to maximize the strengths of the anthropological, open-ended approach to data gathering, in a manner that permits data to be utilised in multi-staged research' (Bentley et al. 1988).	Bentley et al. 1988
Rapid appraisal	Designed to obtain rich data on particular contexts rapidly, pragmatically and in a manner that was deemed more cost-effective.	Beebe 1995
Rapid assessment procedures (RAP)	Emphasised the short amount of time for field data collection, a limited or focused scope of information for evaluation purposes, and the use of a variety of formalised means of data collection.	Fitch at al. 2000; Scrimshaw and Hurtado 1988 Utarini et al. 2001; Harris et al. 1997
RARE	This is an approach that depends on the creation of a team of researchers, normally with community members, the combination of multiple methods and triangulation.	Needle et al. 2003; Brown et al. 2008
Rapid qualitative inquiry (RQI)	Based on intensive teamwork as part of the triangulation of data collection, and intensive teamwork during the iterative process of data analysis and additional data collection (Beebe 2001:7).	Beebe 2001, 2014

the use of local knowledge and expertise. These were one of the oldest rapid qualitative research approaches, emerging in the late 1970s (Manderson and Aaby 1992a). RRAs were pragmatic as they emphasised existing data, use of research teams with a high-level of expertise and research skills, a mixture of qualitative research methods and the involvement of local community members in the research process. Chambers (1981: 95) has described data collection in RRAs as focusing on what was 'relevant, timely and usable'.

Participatory Rural Appraisal (PRA)

Chambers added a slightly more participatory twist to rapid rural appraisals when contributing to the development of PRAs. According to him, PRAs emerged out of the recognition that local community members could make contributions to research and could be empowered to lead on their own appraisals (Chambers 2008). In many of these appraisals, the research was carried out internally, and outsiders were only brought in during analysis or even dissemination stages (Chambers and Blackburn 1996). When comparing RRAs and PRAs, Chambers (1994) has indicated that RRAs were more verbal and active with outsiders in the sense that the main objective was data collection by outsiders. PRAs are more visual and active with locals, and have a sharing-empowering approach where the objectives were evaluation, learning, action and monitoring by insiders (Chambers 1994).

> *Case study:* Participatory rural appraisal of a community-centred response to Ebola in Urban Liberia (Abramowitz et al. 2015)
> The aim of the study was to collect baseline information on community-based epidemic control priorities and identify strategies for containing Ebola in Liberia.
> **Methods**: The study was designed as a participatory rural appraisal across fifteen communities. The study combined fifteen focus groups (n = 368) and observations (communities and emergency-response agencies). The fieldwork lasted twenty days. Members from the communities were recruited to act as research assistants. Thematic analysis (inductive/deductive approach) was used to analyse the data from the focus groups and observations.
> **Findings**: Communities searched for internal resources to deal with marginalisation from public services and assistance and structural violence. When facing barriers to information and care, the communities developed their own triage mechanisms, holding units for those experiencing Ebola symptoms and reporting processes to document cases of illness and deaths. The gendered nature of morbidity and mortality was related to women's caregiving roles.
> **Dissemination and use of findings**: The study was generated as part of a programme assessment and evaluation project conducted by the World Health Organization in Monrovia, in service to the government of Liberia. The findings were used to inform local epidemic response efforts.

Rapid Ethnographic Assessment (REA)

In the late 1980s, anthropologists began to question the amount of time required in the field to collect information on health beliefs and practices. Bentley et al.

(1988: 107) argued that 'anthropologists with long-term experience in applied health care research and planning have become convinced that the process of gathering essential ethnographic data can be a relatively rapid process, and is indeed a necessary response to programmatic time and budgetary constraints.' These authors believed that detailed ethnographic data could not be collected rapidly, but the basic information required to inform health programme delivery could.

REAs were defined as 'a methodological approach that is intended to maximize the strengths of the anthropological, open-ended approach to data gathering, in a manner that permits data to be utilized in multi-staged research' (Bentley et al. 1988). According to McNall and Foster-Fishman (2007), REAs were different than other approaches such as PRAs and rapid appraisals because they used a more limited range of research methods and focused more on exploring the world view and participants' perceptions of health issues.

One defining characteristic of REAs was the development of structured field guides. Field guides provided guidelines for the type of information required to inform health programme delivery. The first guides were developed by Bentley et al. (1988) to collect data on the beliefs and practices related to diarrhoea in children, infant feeding practices, healthcare utilisation, children care patterns and family work roles.

REAs also depended on the recruitment of individuals familiar with the local culture/area to act as researchers. In their application of REAs in Nigeria and Peru, however, Bentley et al. (1988) outlined the difficulties of recruiting local researchers with the required skills to carry out the study or who might be available to work on the project at short notice. Furthermore, not all researchers could move around or relocate to the places where data needed to be collected. REAs have been developed to explore breastfeeding practices in Mexico (Guerrero et al. 1999), beliefs surrounding acute respiratory infections in children (Kresno et al. 1993), family-planning practices among people living with HIV/AIDS in Nigeria (Garko 2007), local attitudes and perceptions towards malaria in Zambia (Williams et al. 1999), diagnosis and management of fever in Ghana (Agyepong et al. 1994), perceptions of childbirth and maternity services (Culhane-Pera et al. 2015), healthcare-seeking practices for ill children in Sierra Leone (K. Scott et al. 2014), perceptions of stroke-like symptoms (Hundt et al. 2004), perceptions of palliative care barriers and facilitators (Goepp et al. 2008), factors influencing antiretroviral therapy use in Thailand (Murray et al. 2016) and caregiver perspectives and experiences accessing childhood illness services (Shaw et al. 2016).

Rapid Appraisals and Rapid Assessments

Rapid assessments or appraisals also stemmed from anthropological research and were designed to obtain rich data on particular contexts rapidly, pragmatically and in a manner that was deemed more cost-effective (Vincent et al. 2000). Teams of researchers were used to collect data from key contacts or informants in the communities. These interviews were combined with other methods such as focus groups, community walks and mapping, and surveys (Garrett and Downen 2002). When possible, researchers used existing data sources and only collected new data if necessary (Aral et al. 2005). Even though rapid appraisals were flexible enough to be used for multiple research and evaluation purposes, they were normally used as diagnostic tools or to capture information from a particular community or specific topic that could then be used to design health programmes or interventions (Desmond et al. 2005; Kirsch 1995; Trotter and Singer 2005).

Rapid Assessment Procedures (RAP)

RAPs were developed by anthropologists at UCLA to improve health programme planning and evaluation by capturing the social and cultural factors that frame health behaviours (Fitch et al. 2000). According to Utarini et al. (2001), *rapid* emphasised the short amount of time for field data collection, *assessment* drew attention to a limited or focused scope of information for evaluation purposes, and *procedures* indicated the use of a variety of formalised means of data collection. Time constraints and the high costs associated with long-term research were some of the main drivers of the development of this approach. Furthermore, researchers believed that community members could make important contributions to the design and implementation of studies and should be a part of research teams (Harris et al. 1997). The distinguishing features of RAPs were:

1. Formation of a multidisciplinary research team including a member from the cultural group of interest
2. Development of materials to train team members
3. Use of several data collection methods to verify information through triangulation
4. Iterative data collection and analysis to facilitate continuous adjustment
5. Completion of the project quickly, usually in four to six weeks (Harris et al. 1997).

One key aspect of RAPs was the belief that the methodology needed to be available to researchers outside of the social sciences and with no prior research experience (Manderson and Aaby 1992a). RAP manuals were developed to guide researchers without a background in disease-based research skills or qualitative research (Fitch et al. 2000). The first manual was published by Scrimshaw and Hurtado in 1987 for their work on primary care and nutrition for UNICEF. It included thirty-one data collection guides covering topics such as characteristics of the community, household and primary healthcare providers (Scrimshaw and Hurtado 1987). I have included some examples of field manuals in Appendix B.

In addition to the limitations identified for rapid qualitative research in general, one limitation associated mainly with RAPs has been the fear that important information might be missing as a result of its structured approach to data collection (for instance, through the use of pre-established manuals). Researchers have expressed concern that RAP methodology might leave little room for serendipity during field-work and limit the capacity of researchers to make changes in the study design along the way (Manderson and Aaby 1992b). Due to its reliance on the use of community members or individuals from the area/sector in question (normally with limited skills in research), potential issues with the quality of the data and reliability of the study have also been highlighted (Harris et al. 1997; Manderson and Aaby 1992a).

Studies using RAP have covered a wide range of topics and generated the following manuals: the evaluation of primary care and nutrition programmes (Scrimshaw and Hurtado 1987), epilepsy (Long et al. 1988), HIV/AIDS (Scrimshaw et al. 1991), the assessment of women's health (Gittelsohn et al. 1998), malaria (Agyepong et al. 1995) and household management of diarrhoea (Herman and Bentley 1993). More recent studies using RAPs have looked at planning emergency services for children (Goepp et al. 2004) and clinical decision support systems (Ash et al. 2010; Ash et al. 2012; Wright et al. 2015). Utarini et al. (2001) have highlighted issues with the reporting of information in RAPs and have proposed eleven criteria for appraising studies using this design. I will come back to these criteria in Chapter 8.

Case study: RAP to inform the planning of emergency services for children in Bolivia (Goepp et al. 2004)

The aim of the study was to explore the social and cultural factors shaping the development of the Emergency Medical Services for Children (EMS-C) in La Paz, Bolivia.

Methods: The research team carried out a RAP based on in-depth interviews (staff and families), small group interviews (staff), participant observation, documentary analysis and secondary data analysis (municipal and national governmental reports, both published and internal; reports from international agencies such as WHO, UNICEF and NGOs) to 'provide rapid information and enhance the likelihood of successful implementation of interventions and services before major investments in infrastructure' (Goepp et al. 2004).

Findings: There were four main factors affecting the planning of emergency services for children in this context. First, the causes of the main injuries were often associated with the emotional and physical effects of poverty. Second, members staff differed in their perception of the 'appropriate use' of emergency services by patients. Third, there was a lack of standardisation of services across medical professionals. Finally, staff identified tangible training gaps that needed to be addressed.

Dissemination and use: the RAP provided valuable information for the planning of emergency services for children and will ensure future services are 'locally driven, culturally appropriate, and socially feasible' (Goepp et al. 2004).

Rapid Assessment, Response and Evaluation (RARE)

RARE is slightly different to some of the other approaches discussed so far in the sense that members of the community/area where the study will take place normally take the first step in identifying the need for research or evaluation. In 1999, the Office of Public Health and Science in the US developed a series of crisis response teams capable of providing training in RARE methodologies to communities affected by HIV/AIDS (Needle et al. 2003). In order for RARE projects to begin, local officials needed to contact the Office requesting assistance. The research team based in the Office of HIV/AIDS Policy met with the local officials to review potential design options, helped put together a local working group and assigned a field research team to help facilitate the assessment. The field research team was led by an ethnographer and carried out an intensive training programme for the local working group with the aim of generating local research capacity (Needle et al. 2003). The use of a structured programme for the training of local researchers was one of the key contributions of RARE to rapid qualitative research.

RARE studies tended to combine focus groups, key informant interviews, observations, mapping and rapid 'street intercept' assessment interviews (Needle et al. 2003). RARE manuals and procedures for data collection are available and can be adapted to different contexts and topics (Trotter et al. 2000). Local working groups played a central role in the design and implementation of the study. They helped review available local data (surveillance, epidemiological, planning data, GIS maps) and identify areas or at-risk groups (Brown et al. 2008). As mentioned before, members from the community/area where the study took place also participated in data collection and analysis. Research teams (composed of the field research teams and community members) met regularly to report on data collection and discuss emerging themes. Findings were also shared regularly with key stakeholders throughout the project. In a study of health disparities in urban disadvantaged communities in Florida, Brown et al. (2008) shared emerging findings with a local group of stakeholders on three occasions over a six-week period (at week 1, week 3 and week 6).

Case study: A participatory action research pilot study of urban health disparities using rapid assessment response and evaluation (RARE) (Brown et al. 2008)

The aim of the study was to carry out a multi-method community health evaluation of two interventions delivered by the Jefferson Reaves Sr Health Center (JRSHC) in the US. The assessment focused on identifying the context where these interventions were implemented and how health disparities shaped healthcare in the community.

Methods: A field team was recruited to carry out data collection. The team was composed of ethnographers, representatives from the community who acted as 'cultural guides', family physicians, psychologists and advanced practice nurses. Three days of training were delivered for the team, and during this training, they developed interview guides and data-sampling strategies. In addition to interviews with key stakeholders, the assessment included GIS mapping of home addresses, an analysis of demographic characteristics of patients, and the frequency of diagnoses and visits to healthcare facilities. The field team met weekly over two months to discuss data collection and assess emerging findings.

Findings: The health assessment indicated that racism and cultural bias were at the root of health disparities in the community. Some members of the community felt disenfranchised and isolated due to language barriers, and both of these factors also contributed to health disparities. Some residents had a tradition of using emergency department rather than primary care and waiting until they were extremely sick to access care. Some discomfort with HIV care was documented, and the reason for this was inconsistency in following complex medication regimens. Rigorous documentation requirements and long waits acted as barriers to care.

Dissemination and use: The health assessment was used to develop a set of targets for health system intervention and resulted in initiatives aimed at improving mental health in the community based on a chronic care model and a primary health promotion programme.

Rapid Qualitative Inquiry

Although his earlier work focused on the development of rapid appraisal methods (Beebe 1995), Beebe (2001, 2004) expanded his portfolio to include rapid assessment processes and, more recently, rapid qualitative inquiry (RQI) (Beebe 2014). Rapid assessment process (not to be confused with RAP above) was based on two main concepts:

1. Intensive teamwork as part of the triangulation of data collection, and
2. Intensive teamwork during the iterative process of data analysis and additional data collection (Beebe 2001:7).

In rapid assessment process and RQI, more than one researcher was always required for data collection and analysis (Beebe 2014). At least two individuals needed to gain sufficient understanding of a situation over a short amount of time (normally one to six weeks), and by collecting data as a team, the interaction of team members added layers of interpretation to the research process (Beebe 2001, 2014). For instance, when using these approaches, the team of researchers would carry out interviews together. By having at least two members of the team present at each interview, they were able to capture different aspects of the conversation or follow up on different topics. The same could be expected when multiple people carried out observations together (Beebe 2014).

Triangulation occurs when combining the data produced through different methods, but in the case of rapid assessment process, triangulation was also produced by the interaction of team members during data collection (Beebe 2014). The assumption was that each team member would have their own perceptions, theories, methods and academic disciplines, which contributed to the generation of a unique world view and different ways of collecting and interpreting data (Beebe 2001).

Another distinguishing feature of RQI and rapid assessment process was their emphasis on iterative data collection and analysis. Data were analysed as researchers were collecting data, allowing the nearly real-time sharing of findings, but also pointing to gaps in data collection researchers could address before the fieldwork was over.

Rapid Evaluations

More than ten years ago, McNall and Foster-Fishman (2007) reviewed the landscape of rapid evaluation and appraisal methods (REAM), documenting the diversity of rapid approaches and highlighting the challenges they shared. They identified an intrinsic tension between speed and trustworthiness and argued that rapid approaches would need to address issues of validity and data quality to gain greater popularity in the evaluation landscape (McNall and Foster-Fishman 2007). In terms of rapid evaluation approaches, McNall and Foster-Fishman (2007) mainly focused on rapid evaluation methods (REM), rapid feedback evaluation (RFE) and real-time evaluation (RTE). A more recent review led by our team has also included rapid cycle evaluation (RCE) and rapid assessment methods (RAM) (Vindrola-Padros et al. 2020). Table 3.2 describes the different rapid evaluation approaches and identifies some key

Table 3.2 Common rapid evaluation designs

Evaluation design	Description	Key literature
Rapid assessment methods (RAM)	Enable gathering of valid and reliable research data within a rapid time frame, and at relatively low cost.	Vincent et al. 2000; Stimson et al. 1997; Pearson and Kessler 1992; Afonja 1992
Rapid evaluation methods (REM)	Set of observation and survey-based diagnostic activities which provide a basis for identifying operational problems and taking action.	Anker et al. 1993; Chowdhury et al. 2004; Aspray et al. 2006; Felisberto et al. 2008; Grant et al. 2011; Munday et al. 2018; Pearson 1989
Rapid feedback evaluation (RFE)	Data are continually collected, analysed and used to inform action within a short time period. Aims to provide programme managers with focused, timely evaluation conclusions.	McNall et al. 2004; Hargreaves 2014; Sonnichsen 2000; Wholey 1983; Bjorson-Benson et al. 1993; McNall et al. 2004; Zakocs et al. 2015
Rapid cycle evaluation (RCE)	Provides timely feedback to funding organisations and programme staff and care providers. Offers support for continuous quality improvement and allows observations of changes over time.	McNall and Foster-Fishman 2007; Shrank 2013; Schneeweiss et al. 2015; Keith et al. 2017; Skillman et al. 2019
Real-time evaluation (RTE)	Based on sharing observations and recommendations on an on-going basis with field staff so as to allow operational problems to be quickly corrected and potential problems to be avoided.	McNall and Foster-Fishman 2007; UNHCR 2002; Jamal and Crisp 2002; Sandison 2003

literature. Some of the more recent types of evaluations are incorporating ethnographic approaches to research, particularly those designed as formative process evaluations for healthcare interventions.

In our recent review, we identified a trend in the design of rapid evaluations, where evaluators are moving away from studies that are short to longer studies with multiple short stages with feedback loops or cycles (Vindrola-Padros et al. 2020). Evaluators are using strategies to speed up evaluations: conducting data collection and analysis in parallel, eliminating the use of transcripts and utilising larger research teams to share the workload. Questions persist in relation to the suitability of rapid evaluation designs, the trustworthiness of the data and the degree to which evaluation findings are used to make changes in practice (Vindrola-Padros et al. 2020).

Case study: Rapid cycle evaluation of a practice transformation intervention aimed at primary care practices in the US (Keith et al. 2017)

Study aim: understand practice transformation efforts led by the Comprehensive Primary Care (CPC) initiative in twenty-one primary care practices in the US.

Data collection methods:

The study was designed as a formative qualitative cross-case evaluation. The study combined the following methods:

1. Semi-structured interviews (five to seven participants per practice)
2. Structured observations using a checklist (one to two days depending on practice size) were used to collect data as members of the research team shadowed staff members

Study scope and duration: The fieldwork was carried out in twenty-one primary care practices over five months.

Research team: The research team was comprised of a medical anthropologist, two primary care physician researchers, two social scientists and several research analysts.

Data analysis methods: Codebooks were developed before coding the data, and refined throughout the coding process. Coding was facilitated by ATLAS.ti. Three researchers participated in the coding and cross-checking of data analysis.

Dissemination and use of findings: following a rapid-cycle evaluation design, findings were shared regularly with the team leading the intervention and used to make changes in the information provided to primary care practices, increase opportunities for peer-to-peer learning between practices and organise learning sessions for practices on how to create care plans with patients.

Reflections from the research team:

- The research team found it useful to create analytic matrices to synthesise the data and identify the findings that needed to be shared with the intervention team.
- Findings needed to be shared with the staff leading the intervention as 'actionable findings' so they could be used to make changes in the intervention.
- The research team organised the findings in a barriers and facilitators table, making it easy for the team leading the intervention to identify the areas that needed to be changed.

The Integration of Rapid Qualitative Research Approaches in Rapid Ethnographies

There will be instances throughout the remainder of the book where I will identify specific tools and techniques developed in the field of rapid qualitative research that have been incorporated into rapid ethnographies. It is difficult to identify where some of these techniques have originated and how they have spread, as there has been a lot of cross-fertilisation across these approaches. Nevertheless, some tangible features that rapid ethnographies might have borrowed from other rapid research approaches include:

1. *The use of structured manuals or guides for data collection*: These structured tools for data collection are often associated with field guides used in REAs or field manuals used in RAPs. Some rapid ethnographies have now relied on the use of these tools to ensure the quicker collection of data. In some instances, these are only used to capture data from observations (Mullaney et al. 2012), but they have also been used to collect data from interviews and documents.

2. *The use of teams of researchers*: Many rapid ethnographies rely on the use of teams of researchers to cover more ground in less amount of time and provide multiple perspectives and types of interpretations during data collection and analysis. Team-based research is a defining characteristic of rapid appraisals, RQI, RARE and RAPs. Rapid ethnographies could benefit from strategies for team-based work developed by these approaches.

3. *Participatory approaches to research*: Some rapid qualitative approaches such as PRA and RARE are based on the use of participatory research processes where members of the community where the research takes place become an active part of the research team. Even though ethnographic research has experimented with more collaborative approaches (Lassiter 2005), the role of the lone researcher and authoritative author tends to remain in many ethnographic studies. The participatory processes used in PRAs and RARE could be changing the ways in which we engage community members in research.

4. *Dissemination and feedback loops*: Rapid evaluations have been the rapid approach that has devoted the most attention to the regular sharing of findings to inform the implementation of interventions and programmes. There are several aspects of rapid evaluations that can be incorporated into rapid ethnographies. These include: the development of a stakeholder group to advise on the research throughout its duration; the establishment of feedback loops to share ongoing findings from the

study; and the use of a scoping study to identify the aims and scope of the study. I will come back to these strategies in Chapter 7.

General Trends in the History of Rapid Ethnographies

When we map out the development of rapid ethnographic research through time, we are able to see that most of the precursory work was carried out throughout the 1980s and 1990s. We are also able to identify a notable increase in the use of rapid ethnographies (using lone ethnographers and team-based approaches) during the 2000s (see Figure 3.1 for the timeline), with a peak from 2010 to the present. Previous approaches, what I have labelled as ethnography-informed rapid research approaches, tended to rely on the use of research teams, structured forms of data collection (i.e. field guides or manuals) and iterative processes to combine data collection and analysis. Rapid ethnographies can also rely on team-based approaches, but have maintained the traditional lone-ethnographer model as a potential design option. Rapid ethnographies have also sought to implement intensive periods of fieldwork, without overreliance on structured tools (as commonly used in RAP or REA). In a way, rapid ethnographies have sought to maintain the essence of conventional ethnography (highly dependent on the use of unstructured fieldnotes) in a way that other rapid research approaches have not.

In health research, the development of these approaches mirrored trends in medical anthropology, beginning with ethnographies in rural settings focusing

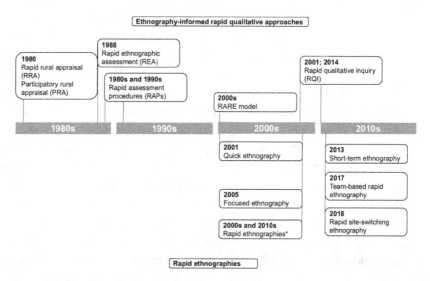

Figure 3.1 Timeline of ethnography-informed rapid research approaches and rapid ethnographies

on folk taxonomies of illness (REAs, PRA, RAPs), moving into cities in the late 1990s and early 2000s with RARE and its emphasis on health behaviours and health seeking practices in disadvantaged urban areas, and ending with an increase of rapid ethnographies in clinical areas in the 2010s, which examined perceptions of care and models for health service delivery.

Conclusion

In this chapter I wanted to present the rich history of rapid research. Emerging perhaps as early as the 1950s, rapid research was first used by anthropologists working in rural environments to quickly assess situations in the field. Anthropologists found that the increase of members of the research team and development of structured tools for data collection were two main ways to effectively reduce the amount of time required for fieldwork. Some of these approaches, such as PRA, also relied on a high degree of participation in study design and implementation by community members. The development of RARE represented an attempt to transfer these methodological innovations from a rural to an urban landscape. The widespread use of rapid ethnographies was not evident until the early 2000s (with notable exceptions such as Coreil et al. 1989). This history is important, as it has shaped the design and implementation of current rapid ethnographies. As we discuss lone-researcher and team-based rapid ethnographies in the following chapters, I will identify different aspects of the precursory work discussed here that has been taken on board and re-adapted for rapid ethnography designs.

4 Rapid Ethnographies as a Lone Researcher

One of the trends I have identified when looking at the history of rapid ethnographies is the abandonment, or less frequent use, of structured forms of data collection like the field manuals or guides used in REAs, and the development of focused but unstructured ways to approach data collection and analysis. More recent developments of rapid ethnographies include quick (QE), focused (FE) and short-term ethnographies (STE). In this chapter, I explore these recent developments in the field of rapid ethnographies, but focus on those carried out by lone researchers. Chapter 5 presents team-based ethnographies. The reason for separating these discussions is that the design characteristics and challenges faced by researchers are different in lone-researcher ethnographies vs. team-based work. The chapter covers the main design characteristics of QE, FE and STE in the form of step-by-step guides, challenges and limitations identified in the literature, published examples and examples from my own work.

Quick Ethnography

Quick ethnographies (QE) are associated with the work of Handwerker (2001), his extensive research experience on entrepreneurship, agriculture and food distribution, and work he carried out for the United States Agency for International Development (USAID), Institute of Development Anthropology (IDA) and the United States Department of Agriculture (USDA). He defined the approach as:

> a package that integrates conventional means of collecting cultural data (like key informant, structured, and cultural mapping interviews), analysing cultural data (like grounded theory forms of text analysis and conventional statistics, and project management (like Gantt and PERT charts) with more novel forms of data collection (like successive pile sorts) and analysis (like the application of multivariate statistical procedures to similarities among informants). (Handwerker, 2001: 4)

The main aim of QE is to develop strategies for collecting high-quality ethnographic research quickly (Handwerker 2001). This can often be achieved by carrying out research in a more efficient way. According to Handwerker (2001), this level of efficiency is obtained by:

- *Creating a clear vision of the aims and objectives*: This strategy entails identifying five focus variables that represent the main features of the research goals. Field tasks are developed in relation to these variables.
- *Creating a clear vision of how these aims and objectives can be achieved:* In order to achieve the aims of the study, it is useful to have a clear picture of when the study will be complete. This involves looking at the variables and identifying when 'an end' in relation to data collection and analysis will be reached.
- *Getting there without getting lost*: The author recognises that getting lost might be an inherent and necessary part of research, but highlights that iterative data collection and analysis and project management skills can help keep the study on track. Iterative data collection and analysis ensure that the data required to meet the aims are being collected. Project management tools such as Gantt charts can help flag instances where tasks might be delayed.
- *Using time to the greatest advantage when in the field:* One way to use time in the field efficiently is to recruit research assistants to help with data collection. The lead researcher, then, acts as a coordinator of the process and ensures data are collected in a consistent manner.

When compared to other rapid ethnographic approaches, QE distinguishes itself due to two main features: (1) an explicit concern with using a theory of culture to address the main problems of ethnographic fieldwork and (2) the representation of ethnographic research as a mixed-methods approach (involving both qualitative and quantitative research) (Handwerker 2001). QE responds to larger debates in anthropology concerning critiques of the concept of culture as homogenous and static (Abu-Lughod 1991). QE searches for variability within individuals in social groups, recognising that cultural differences result from differences in personal experiences, and that culture is in constant transformation (Handwerker 2001: 8).

QE is the only rapid ethnographic research approach that explicitly critiques the equation of ethnographic research with qualitative research. According to Handwerker (2001), research design should be based on the questions the study seeks to answer, and these answers might require the combination of different methodological approaches. A more holistic ethnography would involve questions that require data to be both qualitative and quantitative. Schensul and colleagues, avid proponents of a mixed-methods perception of ethnography, have argued that "both qualitative (defined as descriptions in words) and quantitative (numerical) data are vital parts of the ethnographic research endeavour" (1999: 4).

To date, I have found a few recent studies that reference Handwerker's (2001) work on QE when providing a definition of their rapid ethnography. These include a study in the field of education on itinerant teachers for deaf pupils (Kluwin et al. 2004), studies in pharmacy on overdose (Boyd et al. 2018; Mayer et al. 2018) and Mullaney's (2012) quick ethnography on cancer patients' experiences of radiotherapy. Some authors indicated that the features that distinguish QE from other approaches are the use of a data plan, with identified informants and detailed timelines (Kluwin et al. 2004). This can normally be developed before fieldwork, as researchers tend to have familiarity with the topic or research context (Kluwin et al. 2004).

QE Designs and Step-by-Step Guide

Despite referencing QE, not all of these studies combined quantitative and qualitative data (as originally proposed by Handwerker 2001). However, all studies combined multiple methods and relied on triangulation during the analysis stage. An analysis across published examples of QE points to the steps outlined below for the design and implementation of the approach. It is important to consider that even though these steps are presented in linear sequential form, this does not always happen in practice and some steps might be iterative.

Step 1: Background Research

The limited amount of time available for fieldwork means that researchers need to collect detailed information on the fieldsite and topic before data collection can begin. In some cases, researchers carry out QEs in contexts where they have previously carried out long-term research. In other cases, they encounter new sites and topics and so need to make sure they have at least some background knowledge before entering the field. In order to obtain this background knowledge, I propose a combination of the following strategies:

1. *Brief review of the literature on the topic and geographical context:* examine peer-reviewed and grey literature produced to date using a rapid scoping approach (Tricco et al. 2017). This does not need to take too much time and should only be done to give you a general idea of the topic and context. When focusing on geographical context, limit the review to the sector where the study is taking place, such as education, healthcare, etc. At the end of this process, you can aim to have a few pages with an outline of the main issues that would need to be explored in a study on this topic and this area of the world.

2. *Informal conversations with other researchers who might have worked on the topic or area before:* if you are able to arrange these conversations, these tend to be the richest source of information. Your goal in having these conversations before study design is to make sure you are approaching the topic in the right way (i.e. feasibility of the study) and not replicating work that has already been carried out. You can ask questions about potential study participants to help you design your sampling strategy, any potential barriers you might face gaining access to carry out data collection and tips for overcoming these. You

can also ask about relevant literature to complement the search mentioned above. If you plan to do secondary data analysis on datasets produced locally, you might want to have an early conversation with other researchers who have used the same data source to get an idea of data quality and how easy it was to access the datasets.

3. *Brief review of other rapid ethnographies carried out in the same (or similar) sector:* this review is focused on exploring previous work from a methodological point of view. You can take a look at common QE designs used in the same sector where you will be working to explore which methods are normally combined, how data collection and analysis are organised (i.e. sequentially or in parallel) and any limitations/challenges other researchers might have identified while carrying out this work.

4. *Identification of a theoretical framework/inclination to guide the study:* all ethnographic research, including rapid and quick ethnographies, needs to be shaped by theoretical frameworks. These are the underlying assumptions the researcher has at the beginning of the planning stage that will ultimately guide the formulation of the research questions and the rest of the study.

Step 2: Study Design

The preparatory work carried out in the previous step will help inform the development of the research question(s) guiding the study. These questions will, therefore, be informed by your theoretical framework, gaps in previous research, particularities of your research site/topic and the methodological possibilities afforded by a QE design (meaning that not all research questions can be answered with a QE design). One exercise I recommend to all of my students is the drafting of a study design table. This table maps the research questions, methods of data collection, methods of data analysis and data or information you think you will obtain based on your data collection methods and stage when you think you will have 'good enough' data (see example in Table 4.1). The development of this table will make you think through all of the stages of the study and will ensure that the methods of data collection and analysis you use are linked to your research questions. It can also be used during the implementation of your study to determine when you have collected all of the data you need to answer your questions. You can make this table as simple or complex as you want to (perhaps adding a sampling strategy to it).

Table 4.1 below includes an example of a study design table we developed for a rapid ethnography we carried out recently on the delivery of one-to-one care by nursing staff. The study sought to capture the ways in which one-to-one care was used in practice, how decision-making about this care was made, the strategies used by staff and the particular characteristics of patients who were identified as requiring this type of intensive care. We also sought to

Table 4.1 Example of study design table

Research questions (RQs)	Data collection methods	Data analysis methods	Type of data you think you will obtain	When will you have 'good enough' data
How are decisions related to one-to-one care made on the ward?	Interviews with staff Observations during huddles and team meetings Review of relevant ward documents	Framework analysis	Staff perceptions of how decisions are made (who identifies the case, who has the ultimate say) The negotiation of decisions in practice (instances where there is disagreement among staff about the delivery of one to one care) Barriers or challenges encountered during decision-making The extent to which protocols for one to one care established in ward documents are followed in practice.	Captured the perceptions of a wide range of staff members about decision-making Captured instances when decision-making was not clear and needed to be negotiated Reviewed protocols for one to one care and was able to observe a few instances when these were put into practice (tracked if these were followed as well as deviations)
Who are the patients identified as requiring one to one care?	Interviews with staff Observations during huddles and team meeting Review of relevant ward documents	Framework analysis	Staff descriptions of patients who have received one-to-one care on the ward and their agreement/disagreement with these decisions The discussion of the types of patients during huddles and team meetings and staff agreement or disagreement The identification of 'patient types' and criteria for one to one care in ward documents	At least a few in-depth descriptions of types of patients and their main characteristics Potential issues with these descriptions (i.e. lack of consensus) Examples of how these definitions of patients are operationalised Enough detail to be able to develop a few vignettes of patient cases Overview of how patient types described in documents receive one to one care in practice

Table 4.1 (*cont.*)

Research questions (RQs)	Data collection methods	Data analysis methods	Type of data you think you will obtain	When will you have 'good enough' data
What are the steps/stages involved in providing one to one care for patients?	Interviews with staff Observations during huddles and team meeting Review of relevant ward documents	Framework analysis	Processes normally used by nurses to deliver one-to-one care Variation of these processes (i.e. examples of how these might have varied across the cases observed and why) Staff perceptions of the suitability of these processes and if/how they need to be changed The extent to which the processes outlined in the ward documents are followed in practice	Detailed description of the steps involved in one-to-one care Enough data to provide a few vignettes of how these steps might have varied in practice Overview of the contextual factors that shape how these processes take place Recommendations for the improvement of one to one care Examples of ways in which the steps followed in practice adhere or deviate from those established in ward documents

explore how one-to-one care processes interacted with other types of care processes on the same hospital wards.

In terms of methods, QEs tend to combine interviews, observations, documentary analysis and, in some cases, secondary data analysis. The QE carried out by Mullaney et al. (2012) also used cameras to create patient diaries. The study design ultimately depends on the specific research question of your study. Many rapid ethnographies (even beyond QE) will tend to use interviews (to capture perceptions), observations (to document practices and context) and documentary analysis (to explore a process/issue retrospectively or capture the 'official' versions of a program or intervention and its changes over time).

Another design question has to do with sampling, and this will involve deciding if the study will be carried out at one site or be multi-sited (this again has to do with the research question, but also with the available resources) and deciding the groups of study participants that need to be included in the sampling framework. Handwerker (2001) includes different examples of

Table 4.2 Example of a sampling framework

	Wave 1		Wave 2	
Professional group	Site A	Site B	Site A	Site B
Senior doctors	3	3	3	3
Junior doctors	2	2	2	2
Nursing staff on wards	5	5	5	5
Senior nursing staff in management roles	2	2	2	2
Pharmacists	3	3	3	3
Physiotherapists	3	3	3	3
Occupational therapists	3	3	3	3
Total	21	21	21	21

sampling frameworks (sometimes also referred to as sampling briefs or frames), arguing that the level of detail of these depends on the research question but can at least include variables such as age, gender, class background and ethnic identities. In my experience, QEs tend to be so specific that more detailed sampling frameworks might be required. The idea of using the framework is to have a guide during data collection of the different types of participants or participant groups you would like to approach to take part in the study. The decision of who to include in the framework depends on the views that need to be captured to answer the research question. It is also important to include dissimilar groups, consider conflict and purposely sample 'dissidents' or individuals who might have demonstrated some level of resistance or disagreement.

In health services research QEs, we would normally sample across professional groups, making sure we have captured different levels of training/expertise and clinical areas. If the study involves patients, you might also want to sample patients with different diagnoses, prognoses, age, geographical locations, gender, etc. or other characteristics relevant to the research questions. A generic sampling framework is presented in Table 4.2. It includes the categories of participants that will be approached as well as the target number of people per category, research site, wave of data collection and the total sample size.

Sampling frameworks are also helpful for observations, as researchers might want to observe particular meetings, areas or encounters. A separate framework can be created for these with a target number of observation sessions or observation hours. I also use sampling frameworks for documentary analysis to capture the types of documents I would like to collect. This is particularly helpful for multi-sited research, to ensure the same documents are collected across all sites. It is important to consider that sampling frameworks are working documents, in the sense that they might change throughout fieldwork to incorporate new groups of participants, areas or documents that were not originally considered by the researcher.

Case study: Quick ethnography example: Human-centred design in radiotherapy treatment (Mullaney et al. 2012)

The study aimed to explore the experiences of patients undergoing radiotherapy treatment. Drawing from work in the field of patient-centred care, the study used a human-centred design research approach to identify aspects of care that triggered patient anxiety.

Design: The study was designed as a quick ethnography following Handwerker's (2001) proposal. According to the authors, a quick ethnography design 'enables researchers to gather rich data without direct interaction with the object of study' (Mullaney et al. 2012). The authors combined patient observations, informal interviews with staff, photographic documentation and self-reported materials with patients to collect data on patient interactions and patients' emotional responses to these. The first phase of the study (two weeks) relied on the use of observational methods to map out the patient journeys in the hospital, while the second phase was used to explore patient experience. The study involved observations with thirty members of staff from different professional groups and twelve informal interviews to do the mapping described in phase 1 and observations with sixty-two patients for the second phase. The authors also asked fourteen patients to record their experiences through the use of photo cameras and diaries to document their experiences during the five weeks of treatment. The authors drew from frameworks used in the field of Science and Technology Studies (STS) to analyse the data.

Findings: One of the main findings from the study was that fixation technology used in radiotherapy was a key trigger of anxiety in patients. These types of devices depict the patient as passive and disempowered in their 'sick role'. The authors suggest the use of design to change social perceptions of the role of the patient to that of a powerful user within the healthcare system.

Reflections on the use of quick ethnography: The authors decided to use a quick ethnography study design due to time pressures in the delivery of the study and ethical restrictions posed by the hospital, where the researchers were not allowed to interview patients. They also felt this research approach would allow them to document patient interactions across the different stages of the radiotherapy pathway.

Step 3: Data Collection

Despite a high degree of background work, some QEs include a few days or weeks of familiarisation during initial study stages. Mullaney et al. (2012), for instance, shadowed radiotherapy staff for two weeks to familiarise themselves with the clinical area, pathways of care delivery, staff roles and staff working dynamics. Some QEs might also include one wave of interviews covering general topics and then a second wave of interviews with more specific questions (informed by the findings of the first wave) (Kluwin et al. 2004). Handwerker (2001) also proposes using this time to do a few free listing exercises, where participants are asked a question or given a topic and asked to list everything that comes to mind. This initial period of familiarisation will also be important for building relationships so people in the field can get to know you and get used to your presence.

Data collection can be carried out by one researcher, or local research assistants can be recruited to facilitate the process. One important question researchers face is deciding when the fieldwork goals have been met and the collected data will be 'good enough' to answer the research questions (Handwerker 2001). Sampling frameworks can be used as a guide, but it might not always be possible to meet all of the sampling targets. The last columns (type of data you expect to collect and stage when you think you will obtain 'good enough' data) on the study design table presented before (Table 4.1) can be used to inform decisions about data collection completion. You can ask yourself: Have I collected most of the type of data I listed here and will I be able to answer my research question with this?

Step 4: Data Analysis

Handwerker's (2001) largely quantitative focus makes his description of data analysis methods limited to the search for frequency distributions, relationships between variables, and the identification of intersection(s) among sets of informants. One of the main arguments of the QE approach he sets out is that the design, implementation and analysis of data in quick ethnography should emanate from a theory of culture. This theory of culture is dependent on the labels and names people assign to particular meanings and experiences. According to him, by uncovering these labels we are able to get a glimpse into the world view of our research participants (Handwerker 2001). An important amount of the data analysis techniques he outlines in this approach are related to the management and interpretation of these labels.

Other researchers using QE have placed more of an emphasis on qualitative data, exploring different approaches to coding and thematic analysis (Kluwin et al. 2004; Mayer et al. 2018; Mullaney et al. 2012). Data analysis sometimes involves cross-checking of analysis categories by other researchers (Kluwin et al. 2004; Mayer et al. 2018; Mullaney et al. 2012).

Step 5: Dissemination

Unfortunately, Handwerker (2001) and more recent applications of QE (Kluwin et al. 2004; Mullaney et al. 2012) do not provide information about strategies for dissemination. This represents a notable limitation in our attempt to use rapid ethnographic research findings to inform changes in policy and practice. I will come back to this point later in the book (Chapter 7) arguing that dissemination strategies need to be embedded in the design of rapid ethnographies.

Challenges/Limitations

Some of the authors who have used QE have indicated that despite using detailed sampling frameworks, there are still concerns about sampling bias. Samples in QEs might be more prone to include individuals who are more interested in the topic or have a general interest in research (Kluwin et al. 2004). Most of the quick ethnographies I have found are single-sited studies, which might limit the diversity of experiences the authors can explore and how these are shaped by different contexts.

Focused Ethnography

A later development in the field of rapid ethnographies was the focused ethnography approach. Normally associated with the work of Knoblauch (2005), focused ethnographies have been defined as 'selected, specified, that is, focused aspects of a field' (Knoblauch 2005: 9). Their main features include:

- Short-term field visits
- An interest in a specific research question
- A researcher with insider or background knowledge of the topic or cultural group
- Intensive methods of data collection and recording (i.e. video or audio-taping) (Wall 2014).

Focused ethnographies appeared to be popular even before the work of Knoblauch (2005), and were frequently used in nursing (Roper and Shapira 2000). Some of the early articles of focused ethnographies were published in Spanish (Luduena et al. 2005; Silva and Olson 2005). Those who have used focused ethnographies do not see them as opposed to more traditional, long-term ethnographies, but consider them as complementary. Knoblauch has developed a synthesis of methodological features of both approaches to indicate when focused ethnographies might be appropriate research designs and when the researcher should aim for longer-term work (see Table 4.3).

This comparison appears to be centred on the following dimensions: time (the length of the study, but also how time is used in the field), definitions of the field, knowledge/preparation before fieldwork, and the involvement of other researchers. In the case of focused ethnographies, studies are normally carried out over shorter time frames, but the time spent in the field (and during analysis after fieldwork) is organised in such a way that it can be used to collect and analyse as much information as possible. Similarly, to Handwerker (2001), this might involve developing strategies to make research more efficient, but it can also depend on the use of tools, such as video and

Table 4.3 Comparison of conventional and focused ethnographies (Knoblauch 2005)

Conventional ethnography	Focused ethnography
long-term field visits	short-term field visits
experientially intensive	data/analysis intensity
time extensity	time intensity
writing	recording
solitary data collection and analysis	data session groups
open	focused
social fields	communicative activities
participant role	field-observer role
insider knowledge	background knowledge
subjective understanding	conservation
notes	notes and transcripts
coding	coding and sequential analysis

audio recording to collect larger volumes of data in shorter amounts of time. Videography has been used frequently in focused ethnographies as a way to systematise the analysis of video recordings (Knoblauch et al. 2014).

In a focused ethnography on teaching and learning in conflict zones, Skaras (2018) argues that the combination of video classroom observations and observations in the form of 'hanging out' (Bernard 2006; Bryman 2004), allowed her to capture the different layers of the social processes she sought to understand. Video observation allowed the researcher to capture the curriculum as performed (not as planned) as well as teacher's body language and interaction with students (Skaras 2018). The technique of hanging out allowed access to more informal interactions (i.e. conversations in communal areas), which provided insight into the daily mechanisms used by staff and students to maintain a learning environment in the midst of conflict (Skaras 2018). The detail captured through video observation meant the researcher could spend time in the field collecting other types of data that could not be filmed.

Wall (2014) has argued that focused ethnography can act as a driver for reconceptualising all ethnographic practices. According to her, some topics are not amenable to long-term fieldwork, and many ethnographers work in familiar fields (i.e. topics they have already worked on or research settings close to home) where they do not require the extended amount of time traditional ethnographers need to learn a new language or become familiar with local customs. This pre-fieldwork knowledge, whether pre-existing or acquired for the specific study, becomes a central aspect of the design of focused ethnographies, as it allows researchers to formulate specific research questions, narrowing the definition of their field and designing methods of data collection and sampling strategies that are adaptable to the local context (Knoblauch 2005; Wall 2014).

In a recent focused ethnography on the use of patient engagement technology, the researchers familiarised themselves with the research site and collected relevant information before designing the study (Patmon et al. 2016). The researchers carried out informal interviews with individuals who were familiar with the technology they were studying and used this information to develop the topic guides they used in their semi-structured interviews, identify the areas where they would carry out observations and design their sampling strategy for interviews (Patmon et al. 2016). They also carried out tours of the medical facilities prior to the fieldwork to plan more efficient strategies for the collection of observational data (Patmon et al. 2016).

Several focused ethnographies have been carried out by lone researchers, but in many cases, additional individuals might be brought in during particular stages in research for specific purposes. Knoblauch (2005) mentions the use of researchers to cross-check data analysis (in the form of data session groups), while others have proposed the use of 'member checking' (where researchers might share preliminary analysis with study participants to obtain their feedback on interpretations) (Kilan et al. 2008). Some researchers have also developed team-based approaches in focused ethnographies, but we will discuss these in the next chapter.

FE Design and Step-by-Step Guide

FEs share some of the steps identified for QEs but do not necessarily include quantitative data collection or analysis.

Step 1: Background Research

Cruz and Higginbottom (2013) have argued that FEs are problem-focused, conceptually circumscribed and context-specific. This narrowing of the scope of the research requires either previous knowledge of the topic and/or context or an intensive period of background research prior to designing the study. This preparatory work is essential for making sure the ethnography is focusing on the 'right' things. I have found a combination of steps helpful when doing background research. These include:

- A rapid review of the literature (in peer-reviewed journals and grey literature) on the topic/context under study
- Informal conversations with other research teams that might have carried out similar studies or studies in the same region
- Scoping discussions with people who might become participants during the study (these can be help inform the sampling and the development of interview and observation guides)
- Review of available datasets (if aiming to use existing and routinely collected data)

- Early conversations with potential users of the findings (to identify particular time-points when the findings should be shared, the type of information they expect and the best format to share the information)

Step 2: Study Design

In the case of FEs, data collection can be achieved in compressed study time frames because researchers enter the field with pre-established questions. This means that the stage of design needs to be used to develop and refine these questions as much as possible (Muecke 1994). Roper and Shapira (2000) have argued that many focused ethnographies will use first-level or 'what' questions. This would include questions such as: What are patients' experiences of care during weekends? What are students' perceptions of a new teaching intervention? What are community members' views of the decision to close the local cultural centre?

In my experience, focused ethnographies can often venture beyond 'what' questions to explore 'how' and 'why' questions as well. Ethnographic research is incredibly helpful for documenting processes and practices, so as long as these questions are focused, there is no reason why they cannot be included in focused ethnographies. For instance, Higginbottom (2011) asked internationally educated nurses how their working lives differed in their current location when compared to their country of origin. Kilian et al. (2008) explored how older adults and their adult children responded to potential fall risks (they looked at perceptions, but also documented practices related to fall prevention).

Similarly to QE, focused ethnographies tend to combine different methods of data collection. Most FEs combine interviews and observations, but some have also used focus groups, photo diaries (Garcia and Saewyc 2007) or network mapping methods (Dupuis and Blanchard 2009). FEs are designed as standalone studies or might be linked to bigger pieces of work. Dupuis and Blanchard (2009) report the findings of a focused ethnography that concentrated on identifying the meaning of social engagement for older adults recently relocated to a senior-designated apartment building that was part of a larger ethnographic study on social engagement. The wider study used additional data generation procedures and explored meaning-making in other ways. The FE was used to develop a targeted picture of older adults' experiences (Dupuis and Blanchard 2009).

Step 3: Data Collection

An initial 'entering the field' period is common in FEs. This period is used by the researchers to familiarise themselves with the context, build initial relationships and refine study tools/instruments (Scott and Pollock 2008). Initial observations or interviews might be broad in scope at first to capture general trends or dimensions and may be narrowed down at later stages. Some FEs report using Spradley's (1980) 'grand tour' questions to elicit these broad discussions and follow these up with specific questions (Pasco et al. 2004).

Several researchers have reported keeping reflexive journals or diaries throughout the data collection process (Kilian 2008; Smallwood 2009). These journals are used by the researchers to reflect on their own feelings and perceptions during data collection. These reflections can also be considered data and used to help interpret the study findings.

Some articles report on potential time-saving techniques during data collection. Higginbottom (2011) relied on writing notes after each interview as a way to identify emerging findings early in the data collection process. Ensign and Bell (2004) collected 'shadow' data to enrich their dataset without needing to increase their sample size. Shadow data was generated by asking participants to compare and contrast with others what they know. The researchers asked homeless youth to reflect on access-to-care issues experienced by other young people they knew (Ensign and Bell 2004). Another common strategy was carrying out data collection and analysis in parallel (Dupuis and Blanchard 2009; Higginbottom 2011; Kilian 2008).

Step 4: Data Analysis

The implementation of data collection and analysis in parallel allowed researchers to identify salient topics that needed to be explored further or identify gaps in data collection that needed to be addressed. These salient topics were sometimes discussed in reflective team meetings (Higginbottom 2011). One FE also mentioned the use of participant-checking meetings or interviews, where a selected number of study participants were asked to reflect on the emerging findings from the study (Kilian 2008). These reflections were not just used as a member checking exercise, but were considered additional data (Kilian 2008).

Step 5: Dissemination

Unfortunately, not many focused ethnographies include detailed descriptions of their dissemination strategies. Emerging findings are ready to be shared as data collection is ongoing, as collection and analysis are often done in parallel. Some researchers have reported presenting findings to local teams or hospital units where studies took place (Scott and Pollock 2008). Some of the teams I have worked with have done extensive work during early stages of the study to develop dissemination plans. These plans include understanding the time when findings need to be shared (so they can inform decision-making) as well as the preferred format. Users of findings normally request receiving short reports and face-to-face presentations with relevant groups. We found that the development of visual materials in the form of infographics and animations was also a helpful way of sharing findings (see Chapter 7 for more information).

Challenges/Limitations

FEs share many of the same challenges as other types of rapid ethnographies. However, an issue I have found that is particularly evident in focused ethnographies has to do with study design and the fact that several FEs in the nursing field have only included interviews as part of methods for data collection (Dupuis and Blanchard 2009; Higginbottom 2011; Kilian 2008; Spiers and Wood 2010). The problem is that some of these ethnographies have identified the exploration of practices as part of the study aims. However, if interviews are the only method for data collection, the studies will only be capturing the participants' perceptions of practices and not the practices themselves. Furthermore, this design choice raises wider questions about the definition of ethnography and the types of methods that must be a part of this approach. Does all ethnographic research need to include at least some observational work to get an idea of the local context and practices as described above? This is a question we will come back to later in the book.

Case study: Focused ethnography example (lone researcher): Focused ethnography on social engagement in relocated senior residents (Dupuis-Blanchard et al. 2009)

The study focused on exploring the experience of social engagement in residents who were relocated to a senior-designated building.

Design: The study used a focused ethnographic design involving semi-structured interviews and secondary analysis of observations developed in a larger study. The observations were carried out in a wide range of residence environments and eight organised activities. The researcher carried out interviews with nineteen senior residents. The initial interviews explored experiences of social engagement, but as the data collection and analysis progressed, the researcher added additional topics of discussion based on the emerging findings. At the end of the interview, the researcher developed an ecomap (record of personal social network composition) for each participant. The researcher also carried out one group interview involving eight participants.

Data analysis was carried out in parallel with data collection. The analysis began with open coding, and as the study progressed, the researcher carried out comparisons between the previously established categories. The analysis was facilitated by data analysis software, and the researcher used member checking.

Findings: Senior residents developed four types of relationships: (1) to obtain feelings of security, (2) casual interactions, (3) to be supportive and (4) to engage in friendship.

Dissemination: Not reported.

Short-Term Ethnography

Short-term ethnographies are one of the newest proposals for the development of rapid ethnographic approaches. Pink and Morgan (2013) argued that rich ethnographic research can still be created over short periods of time. Short-term ethnographies require that we undergo a conceptual shift where we identify opportunities for using high-intensity fieldwork to collect in-depth and larger volumes of data over compressed time frames (Pink and Morgan 2013). This conceptual shift also requires a different delineation of the field, similar to the argument made by proponents of focused ethnographies, where the research becomes more targeted. Pink and Morgan (2013) also argue that visual methods (particularly video) can help facilitate data collection during these stages of high-intensity work. Visual methods are seen as a way to engage with participants as they move through their world and capture the flows of everyday life (Pink 2014).

Short-term ethnographies have not been proposed as substitutes of conventional ethnographies, but are seen as distinct approaches to research that can make unique contributions to research in the case of particular topics and settings. Pink and Morgan (2013) set a strong case for going beyond the representation of shorter study time frames as 'limitations', while still acknowledging that not all research questions and study contexts will be amenable to this type of design.

Pink and Morgan (2013) try to distinguish short-term ethnographies from some of the earlier approaches to rapid ethnographic research that we discussed in the previous chapter. According to them, rapid ethnographic assessment (REA) and rapid assessment procedures (RAP) tended to separate anthropological theory and method (Pink and Morgan 2013: 352; see also Manderson and Aaby 1992: 46). Short-term ethnographies, on the other hand, seek to establish a focused dialog between research and theory, delivering findings in a timely manner but also making theoretical contributions to our understanding of human thought and practice (Pink and Morgan 2013).

The practical application of these principles of short-term ethnographies has pointed to the following features of the approach:

- The ethnographer implicates themselves at the centre of the actions taking place at the field site from the beginning of the study (avoiding more passive forms of fieldwork).
- The ethnographer uses past experiences/knowledge to understand what participants are trying to convey or achieve in practice.
- The ethnographer engages in active dialogue with others (i.e. participants, supervisors, other researchers) during fieldwork to help guide the research (iterative approach to research) and engage with theoretical discussions.
- The study includes the collection of visual data to capture rich layers of information, but also to re-engage with the context and materials after the fieldwork has ended and the recordings are reviewed during stages of data analysis (Pink and Morgan 2013).

I wanted to include an in-depth discussion of the steps involved in the design and implementation of short-term ethnographies and the main challenges experienced by researchers, but unfortunately, this approach has not been implemented beyond two published examples (to my knowledge) (Harte et al. 2016; Pink and Morgan 2013). I describe the study developed by Harte et al. (2016) below, but additional work will need to be carried out in the future to explore other examples of this approach.

Case study: Short-term ethnography example: Experiences of childbirth supporters in relation to the hospital-built environment (Harte et al. 2016)

The study focused on identifying the design factors that inhibited or facilitated the practices of childbirth supporters in a hospital in Australia.

Design: The authors carried out a short-term focused video ethnographic single case study of the birthing experiences of one family. The researcher combined video recording of the birth, video-cued interviews with the family and birth supporters, interviews with midwives and observations of the built environment.

The data were analysed using thematic analysis. The researcher analysed text as well as video data through three analysis cycles. The process of watching the video during the video-cued interviews served as a data-gathering technique as well as a member-checking process.

Findings: The experiences of birth supporters were complex and complicated by their limited understanding of the environment and other staff members' willingness to adapt the setting to their needs. Their role was strained between feelings of being needed and being 'in the way'.

Reflections on the use of the short-term ethnography design: The use of the short-term video ethnography facilitated an intensive, complex and rich dataset. It allowed for immersion into the participants' lives without generating disruption.

A Road Map for Lone-Researcher Rapid Ethnographies

In this chapter, I have discussed the design proposals for lone ethnographies made by other researchers in the field. This section walks you through the design and implementation of a lone-researcher rapid ethnography implemented by our team. I have tried to include as much detail as possible, so as to make the content relevant for those currently designing or implementing their own rapid ethnographies.

As I explained in Chapter 1, my ethnographic research on the travel experiences of families seeking oncology treatment in Buenos Aires was organised in three stages: May–August 2008, May–August 2009 and May–August 2010. I originally set out to understand the experiences of children and parents obtaining care after a cancer diagnosis, yet the distribution of medical services meant that many of the families I would encounter in Buenos Aires were from outside provinces. This situation opened my eyes to large flows of patients who needed to leave their place of origin and travel to the capital to access care, and the challenges, hardship and sense of hope associated with these travels.

During early planning of the study, before any data collection was carried out, I followed the set-up stages described earlier in the chapter:

- I carried out a rapid review of the literature on the current situation of the Argentine healthcare system and qualitative research on experiences of paediatric oncology treatment (an example of a rapid evidence review protocol that we frequently use can be found in Appendix C).
- I had informal conversations with two teams in Argentina that had extensive experience carrying out research in public hospitals in Buenos Aires with children with cancer. These conversations were important when selecting which hospitals I needed to include in the study.
- I had scoping discussions with people who might become participants during the study. These were more difficult to arrange in the case of potential patients or parents, but I was able to arrange a few conversations with healthcare workers that shaped the study protocol and the interview topic guides.
- I reviewed a series of published datasets from the national registry of paediatric oncology cases and identified the main areas of the country where children received care, the most frequent cancer diagnoses, and care delivery processes in cases of relapse.
- I had already made contact with a local NGO providing support to the families of children with cancer during my Master's fieldwork. I was, therefore, able to engage in early conversations with them about the potential use of my research findings to inform some their programmes.

After several months of set-up work and making sure I had gone through all of the stages of ethical approval for the study, I was able to travel to Buenos Aires to begin the fieldwork for the first stage. On all occasions, the research was carried out in collaboration with a local NGO that provides medical and other forms of assistance to paediatric oncology patients and their families. I met families in these facilities and they invited me to accompany them on their journeys throughout the city. Through these journeys, I visited the hotels where they stayed, rode the bus or train with them, waited in the government facilities where they requested appointments, drugs and services, and spent time in the places they liked to frequent to have fun.

I used multiple methods to collect data in this study:

- Interviews: I recorded and transcribed seventy interviews (thirty-five with parents and thirty-five with children).
- Four different types of patient drawings: forty-one drawings were made by children and parents, and I recorded and transcribed their interpretations.
- Participant-observation: I followed ten families (included in the original thirty-five) during the last portion of the fieldwork (May–August 2010) and recorded these observations in the form of fieldnotes.
- Historical and public policy document analysis: I consulted four historical archives.

The interviews were organised to obtain disease and treatment histories for each patient, and children and parents were asked to describe their family's experience with treatment and travel. I asked the child and parent to supply information about the technical details of their diagnosis and treatment (i.e. dates, locations, procedures) as well as the series of events that formed part of their migrant experience. In the cases where the family introduced the topic of obtaining non-medical services such as government subsidies, material donations or financial aid, I asked detailed questions about the processes in place for obtaining these. After going over these details, I asked families more general questions about their ideas towards healthcare in Argentina, their advice for other children/parents in the same situation and their reflections on how paediatric oncology treatment could be improved.

I combined verbal narratives with the use of visual methods in the form of drawings. Each child was asked to develop four drawings: (1) One freestyle drawing where the children were allowed to draw anything they wished; (2) Scenes of diagnosis and treatment (I left these instructions vague enough to allow the children flexibility in the interpretation of the terms and the expression of their diagnosis and treatment experiences); (3) Children and parents drew visual life course timelines (these timelines translated life history methodology into a visual form. The idea behind using visual timelines was to triangulate this information with the histories collected verbally. The timelines provided insight into the temporal and spatial organisation of the families' lives and represented a useful mechanism for understanding shifts in already mobile lives). (4) Each child drew the issue or event that had created greatest difficulty for them (I also left these instructions vague on purpose). After the drawings were completed, I asked the child and parent to interpret them and recorded these interpretations. The drawings were used to obtain information on specific experiences in the child's life that created changes. They showed the extent to which cancer diagnosis and migration were conceptualised as disruptive life events by the child.

The interviews, timelines and drawings were combined with participant observation in various settings. The collection of these data focused primarily on the interaction between patients and parents, healthcare professionals and other relevant actors. I kept careful documentation of the daily aspects of life for both children and parents through family activity charts. Ten families (included in the original sample of thirty-five families) were followed through their routines. The information collected from these observations provided a connection between the micro level of patient life and action, the meso level of the institutions they frequented and the macro level of the health and social care system. By keeping track of the activities of children and parents in specific areas, I could obtain a greater understanding of how structures constrained movement and influenced treatment experiences without losing track of the ways in which they conceptualised and reconfigured these spaces according to their own ideas, interests, needs and motivations.

The analysis of the macro level was facilitated by an analysis of historical and contemporary documents to understand the transformations that medical treatment in Argentina has undergone through time (specifically in the last 100 years). I also explored the historical background of contemporary public health policies. The historical research focused on the analysis of centralisation/decentralisation attempts of health services throughout Argentine history and changes in the services provided to oncology patients by the state. I selected these topics because they could provide insight into the current policies, programs and services directed at paediatric oncology patients.

Another portion of the historical research focused specifically on paediatric medicine and the transformations this sub-discipline has undergone through time. The analyses of the processes behind the constitution of the pediatric subject were important for understanding contemporary doctor–patient relationships and the expected role of the child during long processes of hospitalisations. The meanings associated with children and their rights also determined the design of local and global policies concerning access to healthcare and other forms of well-being.

I transcribed the recordings from the interviews and descriptions of the drawings in Spanish and compiled the field notes from the participant-observation into one file. I translated specific aspects of the transcripts to English using selected transcription. I did not have time or resources to translate all of the transcripts to English. Drawing from narrative research, I analysed each child and parent narrative by: (1) identifying all of the actors involved in the situations described during the interviews (i.e. doctors, nurses, other parent, siblings, volunteers, etc.); (2) the main scenes described during the interviews and organised them into categories (it is important to take into consideration that the scenes described by the children and parents were structured by the dynamic of the interview guide which delineated a temporal and sequential arrangement based on biomedical stages: identification of symptoms, diagnosis, treatment, control, relapse, palliative care). Not all of the participants adhered to this structure and many changed the questions to their liking, skipped stages, critiqued the questionnaire and suggested new questions for its improvement.

I used the patterns found in the representation of actors and scenes to create a list of codes. Once I created the list of codes, I reviewed the transcripts and coded them with computer software (Atlas ti). Atlas ti. facilitated the establishment of different types of coding, the comparison of interview transcripts and the coding of images such as the drawings. I also made a list of the topics that were not discussed to compare the issues that did not form part of parents' and children's stories. I compared the transcripts of all individuals according to these codes in order to select the most frequent topics of conversation and to determine how experiences varied among the participants.

I also used the narratives to map out the journeys of each family, their destination(s), places where they stopped and any back and forth between Buenos Aires and their place of origin. The salient topics in children's and parents' narratives were then analysed in relation to the place where the child received treatment, their place of origin and their type of journey. I paid attention to the way in which stories were influenced by the spaces where the interviews were conducted. Furthermore, I analysed the narratives in relation to the larger economic and political context where healthcare is delivered and the biographical background of the narrators (social class, place of origin, gender, age, stage of treatment and medical prognosis). The analysis of this information followed the model proposed by Gubrium and Holstein (2009) performing a holistic reading of narratives where attention is paid to their content and the circumstances behind their production.

The information collected on the characteristics of each household was instrumental in the process of contextualising parents' and children's narratives. These data were summarised into brief vignettes on each family, and portions of these descriptions were used to understand processes of scene selection. The data collected from the reflections the children and parents made regarding the healthcare system, their experiences accessing medical services and the advice they would give to other families were analysed using thematic analysis where the main themes were coded and representative quotes were used to illustrate them.

The drawings were analysed in relation to the audio-recorded explanations made by the children. These interpretations were also coded by paying attention to the general topic of the drawing. The labels used by the participants when describing the drawings were used as the codes in an attempt to represent their voices more accurately. A comparison of the topics of the drawings and the scenes in the narratives was made to see if there were similarities in the issues expressed verbally and visually. The information collected through participant-observation was also transcribed, and the content was analysed using the same codes. These notes were used to situate children's and parents' voices in the relevant context.

I approached each stage as somewhat separate rapid ethnographies in the sense that I transcribed interviews, fieldnotes, drawing interpretations and notes from the documents after each stage, coded and analysed the data and developed a preliminary findings text. All of this then came together under one overarching ethnographic text that would form the base of my doctoral thesis. I also shared findings with the NGO providing support to families after each stage of the fieldwork (in the form of short reports) and maintained ongoing communication with them even after I was not physically in Argentina anymore. This relationship remains until today (more than ten years after my last fieldwork visit).

Conclusion

Three main approaches for lone-researcher rapid ethnographies have been developed: quick ethnographies, focused ethnographies and short-term ethnographies. In this chapter, I have reviewed the main steps involved in their design and implementation and highlighted some of their limitations. I have also flagged examples of all approaches and included a detailed description of the design of a rapid ethnography I carried out in Argentina so you can learn from the experiences of other researchers who have put these into practice. The next chapter follows a similar structure but focuses on team-based rapid ethnographies.

5 Team-Based Rapid Ethnographies

Ethnographic research has normally been associated with a lone researcher responsible for the collection and analysis of data and the development of the ethnographic text. However, considerable work has been carried out to expand and innovate in the way we do ethnographies. Team-based approaches have been used to bring together a wider set of expertise and experience in the collection and interpretation of data (Creese et al. 2008; Jarzabkowski et al. 2015; Mauthner and Doucet 2008). Authors have also called for the need to develop collaborative approaches to ethnographic research, where knowledge is co-produced among multiple stakeholders (Lassiter 2005).

The field of rapid ethnographic research has followed this trend, developing strategies for speeding up the time required for team-based research. The use of teams is not a recent development in the field of rapid research, as some of the earliest forms of rapid qualitative and rapid ethnographic research (i.e. RARE, rapid appraisals, REAs) depended on the use of teams of field researchers to cover more ground and reduce the amount of time required for data collection (Beebe 2004; Needle et al. 2003). Some rapid qualitative research approaches, like rapid qualitative inquiry (RQI), are defined by their team-based techniques as researchers carry out interviews and observations as a team (with each member bringing in their own views into what was said or observed) and analyse data together (Beebe 2014).

The use of teams in rapid ethnographies was not seen as unproblematic, and several researchers have highlighted potential issues such as difficulties training researchers, lack of consistency in data collection and analysis, lack of clarity in relation to roles within the team and an increase in the time required to recruit and train team members (Manderson and Aaby 1992a, 1992b; Bentley et al. 1988; Harris et al. 1997). Despite these potential problems, team-based work has been identified as beneficial, as it facilitates the development of ethnographic research from different points of view, often combining expertise in different fields, areas or topics. Many teams also tend to include 'lay members' or 'insiders' who possess unique knowledge about the topic or context. Furthermore, different strategies such as the development of structured forms of data collection through the use of field manuals or guides, establishment of opportunities for cross-checking during collection and analysis, and creation of tools for collaborative meaning-making have been used to guarantee consistency and greater accuracy of the findings.

In this chapter, I dive into the field of team-based rapid ethnographies. I outline their main features and then discuss three approaches for team-based ethnographies that have been developed to date: team-based focused ethnography, rapid site-switching ethnography and RAPICE (of interest to those working on clinical trials). Similarly to the previous chapter, I discuss the main characteristics of each approach and focus mainly on identifying the steps required to design and implement these types of studies. I shed light on potential limitations and challenges of embarking on the journey of team-based work and provide a few examples of how researchers have used them before. I also describe the design and implementation of a team-based rapid ethnography we carried out recently.

Team-Based Focused Ethnography

As mentioned in the previous chapter, focused ethnographies have been used by lone researchers as well as teams. Bikker et al. (2017) have implemented a team-based approach in the context of health services research. According to these authors, health services research, with a multi-sited study design, many times requires the use of teams of researchers to cover and exert responsibility over particular sites (Bikker et al. 2017). Furthermore, health services research also requires the combination of a wide range of expertise, a need that is addressed with the creation of multidisciplinary teams of researchers (Bikker et al. 2017).

Step-by-Step Guide

Step 1: Background Research and Study Set-up

The first step the authors took, even before study design, was the development of a conceptual review which would be used to inform the FE design as well as the study materials (i.e. observations, interviews and coding framework). The findings from the review were also used to inform the sampling and develop a guidance document for the field researchers.

Step 2: Study Design

The research reported by Bikker et al. (2017) was spread over eight primary care practices in three different geographic locations to study communication technologies. The authors combined non-participant observations of the practices, informal conversations with staff, semi-structured interviews with staff and patients, and document review (minutes of meetings and relevant practice protocols).

The FE team was made up of three field researchers recruited for the purpose of the study and two researchers who led and supervised this work. The field researchers divided up the fieldwork across the eight sites. The team had a workshop before data collection began, to familiarise themselves with the study design and with each other. The team also went through a training exercise during the workshop where they all observed the same setting, compared styles of observation and developed a shared approach. I have used a similar technique in some studies where I have carried out interviews with other members of the team as observers, so we can come up with a similar approach to interviewing.

Step 3: Data Collection

In order to guarantee consistency across researchers and sites, the research team developed standardised documents for participant recruitment and data collection: participant information sheets, consent forms, a case study guide, interview schedules and coding framework. The case study guide was used to make sure the researchers were observing the same types of events or situations (GP clinics, reception, practice meetings, etc.).

The teams relied on teleconferences and two additional face-to-face workshops to maintain team relationships and monitor study progress. They also used these meetings to share emerging findings. A strategy identified as useful for sharing these findings as data collection was ongoing was through the use of 'practice summaries' (Bikker et al. 2017: 5). These summaries were a synthesis of the findings recorded in the field notes developed by the individual researchers. Team-based research entails the transformation of raw field notes to a format that can be used by all members of the research team. In one study where we had five researchers collecting data across eight sites, we used RAP sheets as a way to summarise the key findings from qualitative research, an economic evaluation and quantitative research (Fulop et al. 2019). The RAP sheets allowed us to bring together findings from the three separate streams of work, as well as to compare these findings across the eight sites in a relatively straightforward way.

Step 4: Data Analysis

This process was initially guided by the field researchers. They were the ones who coded data and sent this information to the project leads. A thematic coding structure was designed by the research team and adhered to by the field researchers. One of the leads played a role cross-checking the data and analysis, but all members of the team had some sort of contact with the data and contributed to the analysis.

Step 5: Dissemination

Unfortunately, dissemination and use of findings are not discussed by the authors.

Case study: Team-based focused ethnography example: Focused Rapid Ethnographic Evaluation (FREE) in the study of interactive patient engagement technology (iPET) (Patmon et al. 2016)

The study focused on exploring the perceptions of nurses integrating interactive patient engagement technology into their daily clinical practice in two hospitals in the US.

Design: The authors developed a new focused ethnography design they labelled as FREE. According to them, FREE shares many of the characteristics of focused ethnographies but relies on the extensive use of field notes vs. digital recordings. The study combined interviews and observations with thirty-eight members of staff in two hospitals. The team had informal conversations and carried out a tour of the hospitals to obtain the necessary information to design the guides for the semi-structured interviews, decide the areas that would be observed, design a structured guide for the observations and identify potential study participants.

Data were recorded in the form of field notes. After each day of data collection, the researchers reviewed the field notes to identify emerging findings and areas that required further exploration. Coding was carried out by using a codebook and data analysis software. The analysis process involved other members of the research team to cross-check coding and the development of themes. The authors also went through a process of member checking. Throughout the study, the researchers engaged in a critical reflection of their work, documenting preconceptions and doubts.

Findings: The study participants believed that iPET systems could be beneficial for nursing practice. They acted as a form of distraction for patients and had functionality that affected both patients and nurses. Some of the problems the nurses encountered when interacting with the system could be addressed through nurse training.

Dissemination: Findings were shared once the analysis was complete. The findings were shared with key stakeholders (mainly managers and senior nursing staff members).

Reflections on the use of focused ethnographies: FREE is particularly suitable for studies that focus on human–computer interactions and the assessment of technologies in the work setting.

Rapid Site-Switching Ethnography

I first came across this type of team-based rapid ethnography when I read the work carried out by Armstrong and Lowndes (2018). According to these authors, rapid site-switching ethnography involves at least two researchers, short periods of fieldwork and document review and pre-interviews carried out before formally entering the field (Armstrong and Lowndes 2018). Data intensity is a way to deal with shorter periods of fieldwork. This team carried out a rapid ethnography in multiple care homes (covering six different jurisdictions), and all members of the team were involved in the production of primary data at some stage of the project. The notion of site-switching was introduced to refer to the shuffling of team members across sites, ensuring that site visits included researchers from different countries. The assumption was that team members from other countries could potentially identify factors taken for granted by native researchers (Armstrong and Lowndes 2018). Even though their overall project took several years to complete, of interest to us in this book are the techniques they used to collect and analyse data at each location, managing field visits and the sharing of findings with sites in one-week periods.

Step-by-Step Guide

Step 1: Preparatory Work

Initial team meetings were used to prepare researchers for fieldwork. This preparation was conducted by sharing reading on methods and the research topic. Topic experts were also invited to give presentations. The team also carried out a one-day visit to a care home to get an idea of what a team-based ethnography might look like. The team reflected on what they learned and used these findings to inform the design of the study (Armstrong and Lowndes 2018).

Step 2: Study Design

The team had to make difficult decisions about sampling, so some initial work was carried out with key stakeholders to find out information about potential care homes. Final decisions on sampling were informed by this feedback as well as practical issues such as transportation and level of access to sites. The study design was also informed by a short pilot study, in which teams developed 'wish lists' of documents and areas to observe to see if these would be feasible to access in practice. Interview guides were also developed and tested with potential participants before formal data collection began (Armstrong and Lowndes 2018).

Step 3: Data Collection

The team spent the initial portion of the fieldwork at each care home analysing documents on the context of the care home and carrying out interviews with managers, unions, residents' councils and family councils. This was used to obtain a deeper understanding of the particular characteristics of the care home, but it was also used to inform people about the study. These initial meetings are useful platforms to introduce the members of the research team and give key stakeholders the opportunity to ask questions about the team and the study (Armstrong and Lowndes 2018).

This particular study combined participant observation, photovoice and interviews, but other methods could easily be added in other rapid site-switching ethnographies. The approach to participant observation used by Armstrong and Lowndes (2018) was incredibly thorough and included making sure researchers were exposed to:

- A general tour of the facilities
- Observation shifts starting at 7:00 AM and ending at midnight (to cover different times of the day)
- Observation shifts over weekdays and weekends (to cover different activities happening during the week)
- Flash visit (one-day intensive field visit) at another care home in the locality to act as a comparator (I will come back to this technique in Chapter 8).

Interviews were carried out over these time periods, and some residents were given cameras and asked to take pictures of 'good things worth sharing' (Armstrong and Armstrong 2018: 15). Data collection was carried out in pairs of researchers, and these smaller teams were purposely designed to include researchers from different disciplines, gender, years of experience and country of origin. This was done to ensure different views were reflected in each of the pairs.

Step 4: Data Analysis

Analysis began while researchers were still in the field. During the week of fieldwork at each care home, the team arranged a mid-week meeting to discuss emerging findings. These findings were shared with the sites and informed the remainder of the fieldwork. Data continued to be analysed and 'cut in different ways' after the fieldwork had ended. The researchers used different lenses to make sense of the findings.

Step 5: Dissemination

Fortunately, this example of team-based rapid ethnography contains plenty of detail about how findings from the study were shared. The team used an almost immediate approach to sharing findings, as they provided care homes with a list of 'promising practices' after one week of fieldwork (Armstrong and Armstrong 2018: 17). Findings were also shared with care homes where the team only conducted intensive one-day 'flash ethnography'. The team also shared findings after the fieldwork had ended, going back to most care homes to give presentations. They also held workshops, seminars and other events with relevant stakeholders (Armstrong and Armstrong 2018).

One of the most interesting things for me about this work was the development of a multipronged strategy to dissemination called the 'bookette initiative' (Baines and Gnanayutham 2018: 159). Bookettes were short and accessible paperback books with a summary of the findings. They were made available in multiple formats (print and online) and 'launched' at various public events. Through the 'bookette initiative' the team hoped to take the sharing of findings to a different level, providing evidence to advocates, generating discussion in the wider public and involving decision-makers in debates. An important reflection made by the authors was that the bookette was actually the starting point of a more complex dissemination plan, that snowballed into media interviews, conference presentations, meetings with government and consultations at other care homes (Baines and Gnanayutham 2018).

Case study: Rapid multi-sited ethnography example: Ethnography of market-based solutions for global poverty (Halme et al. 2016)

The authors suggest the integration of rapid multi-sited ethnography into Base of Pyramid (BOP) strategies to study the practices and user needs of low-income communities and develop business innovation programmes based on these needs.

Design: The multi-sited rapid ethnography was organised according to the following stages: preparation, field study, data analysis and the identification of opportunity spaces. The ethnographic research was based on two- to four-week studies conducted sequentially at four sites. The study combined shadowing, photography, video recording, observations, interviews and secondary data analysis.

In order to develop the guides that would be used for the interviews and observations, the team carried out a mind-mapping exercise. This exercise allowed them to create a shared understanding of the aims and scope of the research. Each site was visited by two researchers, but meetings for the entire team were planned in between each site visit to reflect on the field experience and emerging findings.

Data analysis began when researchers were still in the field. Data were reviewed daily. In addition to the field notes from the interviews and observations, the researchers drafted preliminary data analysis memos (with each memo focusing on a specific topic). The process of preselecting photographs also started while researchers were still in the field, as this helped analysis when the fieldwork at all sites had ended. Data were analysed as a team using data analysis software and a pre-established data analysis framework.

Findings: Data were analysed to identify opportunity spaces, that is, areas where the research data might be actionable. The study findings pointed to potential innovation areas for businesses such as taking into consideration the lack of space, RE practices (repairing, reusing, and recycling), developing educational materials and finding ways to give voice to the poor.

Dissemination and use of findings: The findings from the study were fed back to relevant businesses so they could inform market testing and prototyping. The insight generated from the study was generated in a way in which it could lead to actionable outcomes. An advisory board consisting of company representatives guided the study and met quarterly with the research team. A two-day innovation workshop for participating companies was organised by a consulting company after the end of the study. The researchers also participated in the company's post-project innovation rounds.

Reflections on the use of rapid multi-sited ethnographies: This study design was appropriate for situations where long-term fieldwork was not feasible due to time and budget constraints and where user experiences needed to be collected from more than one site. The use of rapid multi-sited ethnographies in this context allowed businesses to co-create innovations, by bringing in their views at early stages and not as testers of already developed innovations, which is the most common practice.

RAPICE

RAPICE stands for Rapid Assessment Procedure Informed Clinical Ethnography. It is an approach developed recently to incorporate qualitative research in the field of pragmatic clinical trials. It combines more structured approaches from Rapid Assessment Procedure (RAP) with intensive fieldwork commonly used in clinical ethnographies (Zatzick et al. 2011). I wanted to bring in an example of the use of rapid ethnographies in a clinical environment and with the purpose of informing clinical practice for researchers interested in doing this type of work. The main characteristics of RAPICE are:

1. Multidisciplinary research team (including clinical expertise and training in ethnographic research)
2. Development of materials to train team members in ethnographic methods and RAP
3. Use of several data collection methods to verify information through triangulation
4. Iterative data collection and analysis
5. Rapid completion (Palinkas and Zatzick 2019).

The aim of RAPICE, and the reason why it is being used in clinical trials, is to collect and analyse data on implementation context, process, barriers, facilitators and perceptions of outcomes. It can be used to answer questions such as: 'What strategies are associated with successful implementation of specific policies, programmes and practices? How do we determine whether these are successful? Why are these strategies effective in producing successful implementation outcomes? RAPICE responds to resource restrictions in pragmatic clinical trials by providing findings at a relatively low cost (Palinkas and Zatzick 2019).

Step-by-Step Guide

The RAPICE designers have divided the procedures for this approach in three main stages outlined below.

Stage 1

The researchers carry out site visits to healthcare organisations participating in the clinical trial. They use these visits to carry out informal interviews and observations. The researchers will normally aim to observe a few staff meetings, clinical procedures and recruitment processes. They will also try to interview a wide range of staff, patients and/or carers. Data are collected in the form of voice recordings for the interviews and field jottings for the observations. The field jottings are then transformed to longer field notes, if necessary. These are shared in relatively raw form with other members of the team at this stage, and these team members provide advice on additional areas that might need to be covered.

Stage 2

This stage includes a more formal analysis process. The method for data analysis depends on the research questions guiding the study, nature of the trial and expected output required for the study. The field researchers carry out a preliminary analysis, or 'first cut' of the data, presenting broad themes to the rest of the team. Team members discuss these themes and additional ones generated by triangulating the data until consensus is reached. The team might decide to continue with data collection if there are any gaps or new areas to explore that emerged during the analysis process. The interpretation of the data might also be shared with study participants at this stage for 'member checking', that is, to cross-check the research team's interpretations.

Stage 3

Palinkas and Zatzick (2019) suggest combining the findings of the rapid ethnography with quantitative data collected on trial implementation and outcomes. However, several rapid ethnographies carried out in parallel to clinical trials have not done this type of analysis. Stage 3 is all about the sharing of findings with the trial team on a regular basis so these can be used to inform the delivery of the trial.

Challenges of Team-Based Rapid Ethnographic Research and Strategies Used to Address Them

Although the approaches for team-based rapid ethnography discussed above are different, several of the challenges identified by the authors overlap. As is common in any type of team-based research, there are concerns about maintaining the consistency of data collection and analysis across researchers. Several strategies are used to overcome these challenges, and these include the development of standardised tools for collecting data (perhaps in the form of field guides or manuals as discussed in Chapter 3), establishment of processes for data collection cross-checking by other members of the team, and development of guides or codebooks for data analysis.

The team using rapid site-switching ethnography developed a standardised information kit with schedules, interview guides and background materials (Armstrong and Armstrong 2018). Bikker et al. (2017) used case study guides to make sure field researchers covered the same areas/situations during observations. Cross-checking loops with other members of the research team were mentioned in all three team-based examples. These were done informally through regular team meetings, where researchers described the ways in which they were collecting data, as well as more formally by designating a member of the team to act as a cross-checker (see Bikker et al. 2017). The role of meetings, particularly those that are face to face, should not be underestimated, and Armstrong and Lowndes (2018) highlight these meetings as one of the main facilitators of their rapid site-switching ethnography. Similar approaches were common in the data analysis phase, with an 'official' cross-checker such as in the team-based focused ethnography or as a more general conversation between members of the team as done in the case of RAPICE.

Another challenge that is not often discussed in the literature has to do with the researchers themselves and the relationships they develop (or don't) with other members of the team. Bikker et al. (2017) reflected on the need to appoint researchers with similar skills that could get along with each other. Armstrong and Lowndes (2018) also alluded to situations where different types of personalities and power relations (permeated by differences in status) shaped relationships between members of the team. Armstrong and Lowndes (2018) had a challenging team situation to address, as their team was composed of twenty-six faculty members and over sixty students over the entire duration of their study. Yet, they also seemed to have been generously funded and could cover the costs of annual face-to-face team meetings (with all international colleagues) and a series of team-building events. It makes me wonder what happens in teams working with more limited budgets. Bikker et al. (2017) described funding some of their field researchers for only a portion of the study and having one researcher continue to the end of the study. This lack of continuity of some members of the team was seen as problematic, particularly during the data analysis and write-up phases (Bikker et al. 2017).

A common assumption is that team-based work is more suitable for rapid study designs, as it is more cost-effective, but the strategies for ensuring that team-based rapid research runs smoothly seem to depend, at least to some extent, on funding. Another issue is that if there are serious problems between researchers, the time pressures might not allow researchers to make changes in staff (as you might expect in longer studies). How do teams who are pressed for time deal with these challenging circumstances or integrate team-building activities and support to address potential problems between team members?

Regardless of funding, one of the key strategies to overcome common challenges seems to be the establishment of spaces and times for team reflection. In the case of RAPICE, for instance, Palinkas and Zatzick (2019) talked about the value of establishing opportunities for peer debriefing and support. Armstrong and Lowndes (2018) have described the importance of team reflexivity, where the team as a whole evaluated their own positionality during fieldwork, discussed potential ethical issues and reached consensus in relation to ways forward.

Another challenge of rapid team-based work that I find interesting lies in the epistemology of team-based ethnographies. Traditionally, ethnographies have been carried out by individuals, and ethnographic fieldwork is seen as a personal, and even intimate, process. Such is the intimacy that many ethnographers do not feel comfortable sharing their field notes with others. There have been extensive debates in anthropology about the publishing of field notes, anthropologists' protection of their own field notes from the public and the potentially harmful consequences for our study participants if field notes fall in the hands of others (Anspach and Mizrachi 2006; Khan 2019). However, team-based ethnographies often rely on the production of field notes by multiple researchers, and on many occasions these researchers will read their notes but will engage with their teammates' notes as well. Some teams choose to redact notes or alter them slightly before sharing them internally. Others will not share 'raw' notes, but will produce an additional set of notes for sharing.

The time pressures in rapid team-based ethnography will mean that researchers will not have enough time to alter notes or develop new sets of notes. This will mean that they will be writing field notes knowing that others will read them or will have to produce summaries of their notes (as Bikker et al. 2017) to share with team members. Both of these techniques raise important questions about the censoring of information and potential loss of detail. Lowndes et al. (2018: 94) reflect on this situation in their book: '[K]nowing that others would read the text made her want to leave out notes when she was uncertain whether she had understood the situation correctly or to drop a reflection that was a bit embarrassing.'

Similarly to lone-researcher ethnography, teams carrying out rapid ethnographies might also encounter difficulties reaching the level of insight that other teams with longer periods of time in the field might be able to obtain. In order to address this potential limitation, teams have carried out pre-fieldwork research, in the form of desk-based research or short visits for familiarisation before fieldwork begins. Others have also made sure that at least one member of the team has extensive experience on the topic and/or geographic area of the research. For instance, Halme et al. (2016) made sure the research team had one departure country researcher and one native researcher, with knowledge of the local culture and language as well as research assistants who were recruited locally during the fieldwork (who were instrumental in helping with translation of interview transcripts).

Richness can also be obtained with different levels of triangulation: more than one data source, more than one researcher, more than one theoretical perspective, more than one method for data collection (Palinkas and Zatzick 2019). As these can be done simultaneously, triangulation at these multiple levels is an efficient way of bringing together additional layers of data and meaning without the need to extend the study time frame.

Another Experience of a Team-Based Rapid Ethnography

So far in the chapter, I have discussed approaches for team-based ethnographies presented in the literature. In this section, I will walk you through the design and implementation of some of our own work, highlighting the decisions made, issues encountered and strategies used to overcome these.

A few years ago, we embarked on the journey to carry out a rapid team-based multi-sited ethnography looking at team dynamics in the case of adverse events in the English NHS. We wanted to understand the contextual factors that influenced team dynamics and how these dynamics varied according to the healthcare organisations where anaesthetists and other healthcare professionals worked. We wanted to know the issues faced by staff and the response of their departments and organisations.

We had a team of three researchers (all of them part-time on the project). Two of these researchers were students (at PhD and MSc levels), and we had some limited funding for research expenses. The project needed to be delivered in one year (from design to final dissemination) to inform a bigger piece of work, which meant we had six to nine months for fieldwork. We knew we needed to capture a wide range of contexts, as NHS provider organisations could vary in their response to these events depending on their geographic location, type of hospital (teaching or district general hospital, rural vs. urban), size, etc. We also knew that we needed to allow for some continuous intensive data collection periods at each site to capture the complexities operating at micro, meso and macro levels and to allow for enough time to capture a wide range of dynamics.

We designed the study to include semi-structured interviews with staff (including different members from multidisciplinary teams, managers and senior Trust staff), observations during relevant team meetings and documentary analysis. We were concerned about access to sites and were not sure NHS Trusts would be keen on supporting a study exploring these topics. As a result, we originally limited the sample to three to four Trusts. We contacted a large number of Trusts that met our study criteria and used the sampling framework below to make sure we captured this diversity of contexts. To our surprise, many Trusts were interested in taking part in the study. We did not have the capacity (team-wise) or the time to carry out intensive data collection across more than four sites, so we devised a sampling strategy where we would keep the original four sites as in-depth case studies but would include an additional four sites as 'high-level' sites (sites where we would only carry out interviews). This was a

Table 5.1 Sampling framework used to select sites across inclusion criteria

	In-depth					High-level		
Criteria	Site 1	Site 2	Site 3	Site 4	Site 5	Site 6	Site 7	Site 8
Geographic location	North	South-east	Midlands	South-west	North	South-east	Midlands	South-west
Type	DGH	Teaching	DGH	Teaching	Teaching	DGH	Teaching	DGH
Rating	Good	Requires improvement	Good	Outstanding	Requires improvement	Good	Good	Requires improvement
Rural/urban	Rural	Urban	Urban	Urban	Urban	Rural	Urban	Rural

compromise in the sense that we knew we would not get the same depth of data in the latter four sites, but we could at least explore some of the more high-level perceived issues across a broader range of sites. After discussing extensively with the team, we felt the benefits of this approach outweighed the need for in-depth data across all eight sites (Table 5.1).

Another concern we had was consistency in data collection across sites and by the different researchers. All three members of the research team would act as field researchers, but these researchers had different levels of experience and different time commitments allocated to the project. I acted as the researcher in charge of providing general oversight over the project and, thus, also acted as a cross-checker of data to make sure we were all collecting the same information. One of the researchers had never carried out interviews, so during initial stages of the study she was paired with a more experienced researcher. I also attended some of the interviews she led as an observer and gave her some feedback afterwards. She has indicated that this support was instrumental during the early stages of fieldwork and it gave her the confidence to then continue with data collection independently.

We used interview topic guides to make sure the interviews were similar and a structured observation guide to make sure we were looking for the same things when we observed meetings. We inputted data into a RAP sheet, a summary of findings in the form of a table (see example in Table 5.2). This RAP sheet was a tool used during data collection where information from each interview, observation episode and document was added to the sheet right after collection. The same RAP sheet template was used by each researcher and across all sites. This meant that by the last day of fieldwork, we had complete tables summarising the main findings for the eight sites included in the study. It also meant that we were able to rapidly share emerging findings when we were only two months into data collection and then again at four months. Both of these were unplanned requests from the study funder.

Table 5.2 Example of a RAP sheet template (used by all three researchers who developed one of these per site)

Hospital code
Location
Type of Trust
Rating
Main types of adverse events identified
Staff definitions of events
Staff perceptions of hospital preparedness for events
Departmental arrangements in case of event
Hospital-wide arrangements in case of event
Description of past events
Individual staff reactions to event
Reactions at department level
Reaction at hospital level
Processes in place for debrief or other types of mechanisms to deal with event after the fact
Staff perceptions of the positive aspects of dealing with these types of events in their hospital
Staff perceptions of the negative aspects of dealing with these types of events in their hospital
Areas that need to be improved
Factors that might hinder/delay improvement
Additional issues/topics not included above

After reviewing and discussing the summaries of the findings, we were ready to develop a codebook for the in-depth analysis of the interview transcripts and field notes. The codebook acted as a reference point for the three researchers so we could make sure we were defining the codes in the same way. As 'official' cross-checker for the study, I also went through the transcripts to examine our coding. I randomly selected eight codes and looked at how we had applied the codes across all of the data sources to make sure these were applied consistently. We then met as a team and discussed why we had used the code in this way. We also met to discuss our wider interpretation of the findings and crafted a series of themes to illustrate the main findings. An interesting aspect of our team was that one of the researchers had a clinical background, one had a social sciences background and the other one had a management background. The variability in backgrounds allowed us to reflect on the data in different ways, enriching the data analysis process.

In addition to drafting a final report on the study findings, we worked with a graphic designer to develop two infographics to summarise the design and main findings from the study. The process of developing the infographics was important, as it forced us to identify the main 'take-home' messages from the study. The graphic designer acted as a distant team member throughout the study as we shared emerging findings with her. She was then able to advise on the aspects of the study that might be more visually appealing and easier to communicate to stakeholders. These infographics were shared with all of the hospitals that took part in the study as well as the funder. The development of the infographics helped us improve our visual communication skills, as it moved us outside of our comfort zone as more text-based communicators.

Whenever I teach a course on rapid ethnography, I ask all attendees to explain how they would make research rapid. I ask them to work in teams and explain their strategies without using text (only using shapes, diagrams or other types of drawings). They are then tasked with sharing their flipchart with another team who have to interpret the visual information without any help from the original team who drew it. I use this to explain the value of good visual communication, but also to highlight how uncomfortable it makes us feel to have to present complex information in this way (as we are not used to doing so).

Conclusion

In this chapter, I have identified three types of team-based rapid ethnographies: focused ethnographies, rapid site-switching ethnographies and the RAPICE approach for clinical trials. Similarly to Chapter 4, I have focused on the details of their design and implementation, but have also highlighted the challenges that emerge when rapid ethnographies are carried out by using teams of researchers. The following chapters discuss the ethical implications of rapid research and strategies for the dissemination of findings – topics that are relevant for all types of rapid ethnographies.

Ethics, Practical Considerations and the Emotional Labour of Rapid Ethnographic Fieldwork

So far, I have discussed different types of rapid ethnographies, highlighting the challenges and limitations particular to each type of design. In this chapter, I focus on a challenge that is pertinent to all rapid research: the timely approval of applications for ethical review. I also go over some of the practicalities of implementing these approaches and the emotional labour of carrying out this type of work.

Procedural Ethics

Some authors have distinguished between procedural ethics and ethics in practice. Procedural ethics refers to 'an approval process requiring adherence to nationally established research ethics guidelines' (Braedley 2018: 40). It is mainly related to the approvals that need to happen locally for the studies to be carried out. These can vary by country and sector (i.e. education, health, etc.). The literature has presented examples of the burden produced by complicated approval processes in long-term research, which warrants discussion of the potential impact of these processes on rapid studies (Green et al. 2006; Silberman et al. 2011). The main reasons for these delays reported to date have been burdensome bureaucratic processes, approval processes designed for clinical trials and not applicable to other types of research (including unfamiliarity with qualitative research) and lack of researcher training in obtaining approvals (Driscoll et al. 2008; Iedema et al. 2012; Polito et al. 2014).

Delays can be further exacerbated by the requirement to seek approvals from different organisations in order to carry out research (Fudge et al. 2010; Mallick and O'Callaghan 2009; Silberman and Kahn 2011; Petersen et al. 2012). I have reflected on the approval processes for a recent low-risk ethnographic study in the English National Health Service (NHS) and how long it took us to obtain the approvals at each stage. We began developing the materials (including the study protocol) in month 0 and had applied for sponsorship approval at our local research office by month 2. This approval process took one month, and we were then able to submit an application to the Health Research Authority (HRA) for national approval. This approval process took one month. After HRA approval, we needed to seek approval at the local research offices of the hospitals where we would be working. The study would take place in four NHS Trusts, and even though the paperwork was all submitted at the same time, the local approval dates varied significantly. The first two approvals were relatively quick and painless, with site 1 approving in one month and site 2 in two months. Site 3 asked for additional documentation, even though this was not requested in the previous two sites (leading to approval in three months). Site 4 was delayed, as the person who had originally agreed to be our local contact had then decided they did not have time to fulfil this role. Approval at the last site was significantly delayed and was not obtained until seven months after originally submitting the documentation. We still started data collection at the other sites, but had to request an extension to finish fieldwork at the last site.

Even after the local approvals at hospitals were obtained, all researchers going into the sites needed to have letters of access (LoA) issued by the local research offices to carry out data collection on-site. In order for the LoAs to be issued, the researchers needed a research passport: a form that requires sign-off from the university human resources department, local department coordinator, line manager and occupational health specialist. The main reason for delay in our department was the occupational health sign-off, as appointments to see a member of staff were being issued with a delay of at least two months. The idea behind research passports is that these should allow researchers to obtain LoAs at NHS Trusts quickly without requiring additional checks or documentation. In the case of our study, this was true for three of the four hospitals, as one hospital requested a certificate for a training course that had not been identified as a requirement in the research passport or by the research offices in the other hospitals.

In sum, despite attempts to streamline ethical approval processes in the UK, the process continues to be burdensome and lengthy for low-risk studies. How do researchers experience these processes when attempting to carry out rapid research? In our review on the use of rapid ethnographies in healthcare (Vindrola-Padros and Vindrola-Padros 2018), we did not find any reported delays in ethical approval processes, even when some of the study time frames were short. This could be due to lack of reporting, but it does flag a potential area of future exploration to determine if ethical review committees are becoming more responsive to the time-sensitive requirements of rapid research (McDonach et al. 2009). In our own work, we are aware of at least three main mechanisms used to streamline approvals for ethnographic research: classification as service evaluation; separate approval processes for low-risk studies; and fast-track or accelerated approval processes for a selection of studies.

In the case of our rapid studies, three of these have been classified as service evaluations, which meant that the documentation was submitted to our local (university) research office, classified as service evaluation and then registered locally as a service evaluation in the hospitals where the research took place (without requiring extensive local approval processes). This process lasted anywhere from one to two months for single-sited as well as multi-sited studies. Not all studies can be classified as a service evaluation, and there are certainly benefits of going through more formal ethical approval processes. Furthermore, some journals are refusing to publish study protocols and research articles from service evaluations.

Most research ethics committees have developed separate processes for low-risk studies, which might mean that an application does not need to be reviewed by a full ethics committee, but can sometimes be reviewed by a sub-committee or the Chair. Institutional review boards (IRBs) in the US refer to this type of review process as expedited (Millum and Menikoff 2010). This means that applications are reviewed on an ongoing basis and researchers do not need to wait for a full committee meeting, saving time. This option is normally offered to low-risk studies, which refers to those that do not include data collection with vulnerable populations (i.e. children, people who are imprisoned, have reduced capacity for consenting to take part in the study, etc.) or involve some type of clinical intervention.

Regardless of these options, ethical approval processes continue to be a source of stress and delay in the implementation of rapid research. They also have an impact on the financial resources of research teams who might need to recruit staff with the specific purpose of navigating the approval process landscape (Braedley 2018: 41) or might need to extend study timelines due to delays. Some of the rapid ethnographies I reviewed for this book had identified strategies that had been helpful in circumventing some of the barriers in ethical approval. A clear strategy has to do with planning and including ethical approvals as part of the study timeline. This will also imply carrying out as many approval processes as possible in parallel. For instance, in the case of a recent study, we applied for HRA approval at the same time as ethical approval at our university, and while researchers were undergoing the required checks for their research passports. We calculated that this saved us at least three months.

Other teams have proposed including 'ethics veterans' in research teams (Braedley 2018): experienced members of the team who can help anticipate potential problems, develop strategies for parallel processes as described above, and address issues identified by ethics committees in a timely way. Ultimately, researchers who are pressed for time might need to exclude research activities and participant populations considered high risk or problematic by research ethics committees, or might need to limit the number of sites included in the studies (see examples of this in relation to the exclusion of photography as a data collection method in Armstrong and Lowndes 2018, and the decision to omit patient interviews in Mullaney et al. 2012). This is unfortunate, as it ends up limiting the type of research that can be carried out rapidly.

Do We Need to Change Procedural Ethics Processes for Rapid Research?

An argument could be made in favour of establishing separate ethical review processes for research that is deemed to be time-sensitive. For instance, a framework has been proposed by Tansey et al. (2010) for research on emergencies, where ethical approvals need to be obtained quickly. The authors have argued that this framework requires a combination of speed, depth and proportionality (Tansey et al. 2010). These features would be guaranteed by the following processes:

1. Relevant protocols are prioritised to facilitate review within hours of receipt.
2. Not all protocols are reviewed in the same way, with more time allocated to protocols considered more 'high-risk'.
3. A streamlined format for communicating with researchers is established to reduce time.
4. Committee members only review protocols where they have relevant expertise.
5. Face-to-face meetings are not required and can be carried out virtually.
6. Heightened monitoring can be proposed for studies deemed 'high-risk' (Tansey et al. 2010).

The ethics review board (ERB), an independent ethics committee that reviews studies carried out by non-governmental organisations such as Medecins Sans Frontieres (MSF) that can be considered time-sensitive, has also established its own ethical review framework (Schopper et al. 2009). Recent publications have explored how this framework has been used to streamline or facilitate ethical review processes for some types of research (Schopper et al. 2015). Analyses of data routinely collected by MSF has currently been considered exempt from ERB approval (provided patients and/or staff have been informed about how it will be used, no patient identifiers are revealed, harm is minimal, benefits to the programme and community are described and regulatory requirements from the country where the data originate are followed). In addition, not all surveys are reviewed by the ERB, as only those covering sensitive topics or where questions are added to or removed from standard protocols need to be submitted to the board (Schopper et al. 2015).

In the case of emergencies, the ERB has adopted a type of review of 'generic' research protocols, which can be submitted for approval before the research location is known (Schopper et al. 2015). Once the location is known, a final protocol needs to be submitted, but approvals can be carried out by the Chair and two committee members within forty-eight hours of submission (Schopper et al. 2015). This process has been used on several occasions during the Ebola outbreak (Schopper et al. 2015).

It is still unclear to me if we need to add new fast-track approval processes for rapid research or if it is better to focus our energy on improving the speed and efficiency of existing ones. This will need to be an area of future development for the field of rapid research.

Ethics in Practice

Ethics in practice refers to the emergence of ethical dilemmas in the production of research, through all stages of implementation and dissemination of study findings (Braedley 2018). Considerable work has been carried out to explore these potential dilemmas in ethnographic research (Fluehr-Lobban 1991; LeCompte and Schensul 2015; Whiteford and Trotter 2008), so my aim in this section is not to duplicate these discussions, but to highlight the potential ethical dilemmas that might emerge in an ethnographic study that is carried out rapidly.

One of the potential ethical issues identified in research in time-sensitive contexts has been the low quality of the informed consent process. Whenever I teach about rapid ethnographies, I always argue that these should follow the same ethical principles as conventional ethnographies, seeking informed consent from participants, maintaining voluntary participation in research and guaranteeing anonymity and confidentiality. In all of my courses, I stress that rapid ethnography does not require that we modify any of these principles for the sake of completing a study within a shorter time frame. I would never recommend rushing a potential participant's decision to take part in a study. Instead, our teams would normally seek to speed up other aspects of the research to allow the same amount of time for potential participants to read the information sheets and ask questions (the standard tends to be about forty-eight hours). We might also need to see informed consent as a process (instead of a one-off event) and confirm consent to take part in the study on several occasions. This might be particularly relevant for rapid ethnographies where data collection is an intensive and, potentially, burdensome process for participants.

Furthermore, we would maintain the same level of security for data management and storage that we would use for any longer study, using encrypted voice recorders and storing data on secure servers. Early planning stages, during which the infrastructure for the study implementation is set up, are instrumental in ensuring that we do not 'cut corners' when carrying out the study. These planning stages involve the set-up of secure drivers, transcription company contracts, and the purchase of recording equipment that will allow us to manage the data properly. These stages are also used to make sure the members of the research team have undergone the necessary training on potential ethical issues that might emerge throughout the study (including potential issues related to information governance).

Another issue that can emerge is in relation to the responsibility over the findings, particularly if the research is carried out rapidly in order to inform important decisions that might affect those who have taken part in the study. Chapter 7 focuses on the dissemination and use of findings, but it is important to discuss this issue in relation to the ethical dilemmas that might emerge if a study is designed rapidly but findings are not shared in a way in which they can be 'actionable'. In a review of ethical guidelines used in the context of natural disasters and humanitarian crises, Mezinska et al. (2016) have found that some guidelines have established post-research obligations for researchers, including the feedback of results to participants and the general public, and the sharing of the benefits of the research downstream in the form of the development of new interventions or intellectual property. I explore the responsibility over study findings in greater detail in the vignette below.

Vignette: When you decide not to proceed with a study

I worked as part of a multidisciplinary research team that actively collaborated with clinical teams to develop joint research projects. We spent time on several hospital wards, interviewing and observing staff to identify ways in which their working conditions could be improved. We were approached by a group of hospital managers tasked with the responsibility of improving the quality of care in a selected number of wards identified as 'problematic'.

The hospital managers wanted us to help them develop and evaluate a series of audits aimed at improving care delivery. When looking at the data the managers wanted to collect, it was evident that the purpose of the audits was to track individual staff members' use of time, errors and deviations from 'standard' practice. In other words, the audits were to serve as a performance management tool that would have direct consequences on the working experience of clinical staff. The audits were also framed under a punitive system whereby staff would be reprimanded if they did not adhere to standards.

We met on several occasions to discuss this potential research project and consistently pointed to the other type of impact the research could have: the negative consequences on staff working experiences. We drew from examples and contextual information obtained after a long period of engagement with clinical teams and our knowledge of internal political processes taking place in the hospital to show the managers the unintended, or at least undisclosed, consequences of the audit system. The clinical staff would be penalised for actions that not always depended on individual decisions and were often influenced by faulty management processes established at other levels of the organisation.

After a series of team meetings, we met with the group of managers to express our concerns about the repercussions of the new audits, and indicated the team's inability to take part in the project. We continued to work with clinical teams and management staff and tried to salvage working relationships that might have been affected by our unwillingness to participate in the audit project. The hospital implemented a modified version of the audit system and will work towards conducting an internal evaluation of the effectiveness of the audits in the next year. The evaluation will take into consideration the experiences of staff with the new system. The push towards translating research findings into changes in practice can sometimes be obfuscating and not let us see the unintended consequences of our research. The desire to prove that the study can have a direct impact often outweighs critical considerations of our involvement as researchers. Looking back, I think we made the right decision, but the multiple meetings, difficult conversations and our inability to convince hospital managers to change the audit system were all factors that had a negative emotional effect on our team.

This case was first discussed in Baim-Lance and Vindrola-Padros (2015).

Emotional Labour in Rapid Ethnographies

When we read about ethnographic research, we do not always get an idea of the emotional impact of the research on the ethnographer. This is true for conventional as well as rapid ethnographies, but, as fieldwork for rapid ethnographies is often condensed and intensified to collect more data/cover more ground in a shorter amount of time, I think this topic warrants brief discussion in this chapter.

When Pink and Morgan (2013) made their proposal to intensify fieldwork, they were probably picturing data collection processes where the ethnographers would immerse themselves in the field, trying to engage fully in daily activities to capture a wide range of situations in a short amount of time. Depending on the topic, this could mean researchers are in direct contact with potentially distressing situations without having the option to schedule breaks from fieldwork. For instance, I have carried out both long-term and rapid research with patients receiving end-of-life care and their families. In long-term studies, I have always been able to space out data collection so I have some days of the week where, instead of being directly in the field (i.e. hospital, hospice or participant's home), I remove myself from these locations to work on the development of my field notes or carry out some other form of data collection (documentary research, for example). I have valued this time to take a step back, reflect and prepare myself at an emotional level for the fieldwork that is yet to come.

In rapid ethnographies on the same topic, however, I seldom have the opportunity to do this. Every day in the field is precious, and data collection is, therefore, intensified to capture the experiences of more patients or different types of situations or contexts. Even though some breaks in the field might still be possible or might emerge naturally if we are experiencing delays gaining access, the more 'efficient' framing of rapid ethnographic research tends to push us towards a data collection frenzy, sometimes without acknowledging the emotional toll it might have on the researcher. If we are able to recognise the emotional labour involved in rapid ethnographic research and anticipate situations that might be particularly difficult for researchers to deal with, then, from an early design stage, we can build in periods during data collection to give researchers a break or allow them to receive support in the form of counselling. This is important in the case of researchers working on sensitive or emotionally draining topics, but it could be relevant for all researchers working on rapid ethnographies. We have now built a dynamic form of counselling into our project management to make sure all researchers are supported throughout the studies. The pressure to complete a study in a short amount of time should not be taken for granted, and many researchers might find they are not able to deal adequately with these levels of stress. Rapid research is difficult, so we also need to take into consideration situations in which researchers might attempt rapid ethnographies and fail, requiring extensions or abandoning the study completely. The potential frustration experienced in these cases needs to be addressed by individual researchers and within teams. I have included a short vignette on my own experience of failure to further exemplify this point, which follows.

Vignette: When your study fails

A few years ago, we were approached by a team in a Latin American country to carry out a rapid ethnography of a telemedicine nursing service. The service was being implemented to address issues with nursing vacancies in some areas of the country and the unequal distribution of professional expertise. Through virtual meetings facilitated by a teleconference platform, nursing staff in the more deprived areas of the country could obtain access to a panel of experts who could advise on complex patient cases. We were asked to develop a study that could capture the complexities of local care in sites that were suffering from workforce issues, the impact of staff and expertise shortage on patient care and the potential impact of the new telemedicine service.

We were very interested in the study, as it was aligned to the expertise and research interests of several members of the team. Furthermore, the research had the potential to inform the development of the telemedicine service. We designed a study protocol and relevant study materials, obtained ethical approvals and set up a research team (which meant developing an international team, as the service was being rolled out in Latin America). We arranged a series of international teleconferences, bringing together our research team in the UK, the research team who would be in charge of data collection, the service designers and implementers, and stakeholders from the department of health of the country where the service was to be implemented.

Data collection was scheduled to begin in two weeks, and at that time we started hearing concerns from members of the team in relation to potential issues with obtaining access to carry out interviews and observations. The issues were produced by the fact that service leads in several of the sites had decided to block access to areas in the hospital that needed to be observed and had instructed staff in these hospitals to refuse participation in the study. Despite engaging with service leads early in the process and co-designing the study protocol with them, there were evident internal politics that prevented us from gaining access and not much we could do to negotiate these.

Our teams attempted to gain access through various mechanisms for six more weeks, until it became evident that the study could not move forward. It was a highly emotional and draining experience for many of those involved. The teams based at the research sites had to have difficult conversations with people they had worked with before, in some cases creating irreparable damage. We tried to support the process as much as possible at a distance, and I travelled to have a few important conversations face to face. Eventually, we had a team meeting where we decided to withdraw the request for access to the sites and inform the relevant research ethics committees that the study would not be recruiting any participants. We tried to use the experience as a learning opportunity, but I think the emotional toll it had on several team members should not be underestimated.

Practicalities and Tips

Whenever I teach about rapid ethnographies, I always get asked about quick tools or tips for data collection and analysis that can be used to speed up the research process. As a result of this demand and our own interest in the topic, a colleague and I decided to carry out a systematic review examining the tools and techniques currently being used in rapid qualitative research (Johnson and Vindrola-Padros

2020). We found eighteen articles describing some sort of rapid tool or technique. These rapid techniques were used mainly to: (1) reduce time, (2) reduce cost, (3) increase the amount of collected data (due to the reduction of time required to collect it), (4) improve efficiency, (5) improve accuracy and (6) obtain a closer approximation to the narrated realities of research participants. The need to reduce the time for research featured across most articles, but some techniques, such as the analysis of interview recordings, were also focused on reducing the errors and interpretation biases produced by transcription. Mind-mapping techniques were also used to improve the accuracy of the research by allowing participants to cross-check interpretations in real time as the mind maps were developed.

In the case of techniques related to transcription, we found two main ways in which methods were adapted to suit rapid time frames: (1) eliminate the creation of transcripts altogether or (2) speed up the process of creating transcripts. The first theme involved bypassing the creation of time-consuming transcripts through simultaneous collection and analysis of data (e.g. mind mapping) or by coding data directly from its audio/visual source – or a combination of both (Burguess-Allen and Owen-Smith 2010; Gravois et al. 1992; Halcomb et al. 2006; Markle et al. 2011; Neal et al. 2015; Petro 2010; Tattersall and Vernon 2007). Authors tended to describe direct coding of either full or selected segments of audio from interview/discussion sessions.

The majority of articles we reviewed preferred to eliminate the transcript production phase entirely; however, we found some articles which still privileged the creation of verbatim transcripts prior to coding and analysing text-based data (Scott et al. 2009; Johnson 2011; Anderson 1998; Park and Zeanah 2005). This second group of articles involved the use of specialised equipment (e.g. voice recognition software) or persons with specialised knowledge and equipment (e.g. court reporters or scribes) to speed up the process of creating transcripts prior to beginning data analysis. One article relied on the use of transcripts but proposed a method for data analysis based on the use of tables and spreadsheets to undergo a 'data reduction' process (Watkins 2017). All of the articles we looked at prioritised either eliminating or speeding up the process of transcribing data in order to adapt more traditional data collection and analysis methods for a rapid time frame (Table 6.1).

Not many of these rapid techniques have been evaluated, but when we found evaluations, rapid techniques tended to yield similar findings to more traditional approaches. In the case of mind mapping, the evaluation findings indicated that this technique generated the same 'broad' themes as more traditional methods, with the added benefit of allowing participants to be a part of the analysis process (Burgess-Allen and Owen-Smith 2010). Gravois et al. (1992) similarly concluded that the reliability of coded data from transcripts and direct coding from audio fell within the range of 'acceptable reliability.' Three recent articles

Table 6.1 Rapid techniques used in qualitative research

Description of rapid technique	Research stage	References
Direct coding from audio recordings (bypassing transcription)	Data analysis	Gravois et al 1992.; Neal et al. 2015; Greenwood et al. 2017; Markle et al. 2011; Halcomb et al. 2006
Voice recognition software	Data analysis	Anderson 1998; Park and Zeanah 2005; Johnson 2011
Mind mapping	Data analysis	Tattersall and Vernon 2007
Use of court reporters for real-time transcription	Data collection	Scott et al. 2009
Mind mapping	Data collection and analysis	Burgess-Allen and Owen-Smith 2010; Petro 2010
Combination of field notes, transcripts and tape recordings	Data collection and analysis	Tessier 2012
Rapid usability analysis	Data collection	Lopez et al. 2017
Data reduction process	Data analysis	Watkins 2017
Comparison of rapid data analysis with thematic analysis	Data analysis	Taylor et al. 2018; Gale et al. 2019
The use of scribes to record interview data	Data collection	Eaton et al. 2019

Source: Vindrola-Padros and Johnson (2020).

compared the findings obtained from analysis based on direct coding from focus group recordings with coding from transcripts (Greenwood et al. 2017) and rapid and 'traditional' analysis techniques using the same dataset (Gale et al. 2019; Taylor et al. 2018). All three comparative studies found that rapid techniques generated similar findings to 'traditional' techniques, but required experienced researchers.

The findings are slightly different when evaluating voice recognition software. Two articles used an evaluation technique on transcripts produced via voice recognition software, where direct side-by-side comparisons were made between a selection of data using the traditional listen-and-type method and the software-produced transcripts. Johnson (2011) did not find an increase in transcription speed with voice recognition software, but indicated that it might ease physical and mental stress normally associated with the listen-and-type method of transcription. Park and Zeanah (2005) also found that voice recognition software led to the creation of transcripts in a comparable time to transcripts developed by a competent typist, but highlighted the software might be useful for slow typists or researchers with disabilities.

The benefits of using these techniques described by the majority of articles – beyond the obvious reduction in time between data collection and analysis – included the ability to collect more data and include more research participants (due to the reduction in time), decrease the cost of research, provide greater insight into data beyond what can be learned from reading a transcript/maintaining non-verbal information (e.g. pauses in speech, volume fluctuations), potentially eliminate the interpretative bias in creating a transcript, limit the opportunity for human error, increase the 'authenticity' or 'link' with data, create a better match between theory and design, increase physical comfort during data analysis and enhance transparency of the data analysis process (for full list of benefits per article, see Appendix D).

The articles we reviewed reflected on the limitations of using these rapid techniques. These included reduction in the natural pace of group discussions and/or reduced interaction with the facilitator to allow time for charting data during data collection (i.e. mind mapping), potential for not achieving the same 'depth' or 'level of interpretation' as traditional data analysis methods, greater possibility of introducing researcher bias (e.g. by editing audio/video footage in a way which distorts original intent), use of method which may still require (selective) use of transcripts and/or use of other methods, additional time required to master new technologies and/or 'unlearn' a previous methodology, cost to purchase new technologies, potential loss of data if coding directly from audio, reliance on experienced researchers to obtain the same quality of findings as when using 'traditional' analysis techniques, required hiring of a specialty profession that may not be available in rural areas (i.e. court reporter), lack of sophistication of voice recognition software requiring additional time burdens (e.g. proofreading, adding punctuation), and voice fatigue during dictation.

Several of the articles we looked at caution that rapid techniques do not supplant the use of more traditional methodologies. Key recommendations for the use of rapid techniques, beyond a more rapid time frame for data collection and analysis, include its applicability for applied research settings (due to methodological adaptations to the data collection process) and its ability to generate consensus among a diverse group of research participants and/or stakeholders with 'divergent' viewpoints. However, these techniques are not appropriate for all research settings; they will require methodological adaptations that may call for (at a minimum) multiple team members, some of which should be experienced researchers, to deploy methodological innovations successfully and a willingness on the part of qualitative researchers to engage with new methodologies and technologies.

An unexpected finding that emerged from the review were arguments that favoured coding recordings, not only to speed up the research, but to guarantee the accuracy and richness of interpretation. The process of transcription, which is often taken for granted in qualitative research, was brought under scrutiny by several authors, as the methodology used to produce those transcripts has a direct impact on the nature of data to be analysed. As Markle et al. (2011) argued, 'transcription is never theory-neutral.' One important lesson we can learn from this review is to be transparent and critical about the processes used to transcribe recordings.

Conclusion

In this chapter, I have attempted to give a brief overview of current ethical review processes and their limitations when dealing with rapid studies. I have also explored the potential ethical dilemmas that might emerge in rapid ethnographies and the strategies other researchers have developed to address them. I end the chapter with a discussion of the emotional labour involved in rapid ethnographies, recognising the emotional impact of carrying out intensive fieldwork, dealing with time pressures and failing to implement the study on individual researchers and teams.

7 Dissemination and the Use of Findings

For those of us doing applied research, it is important to learn about how to disseminate research findings to guarantee their use. Unfortunately, our reviews on the use of rapid ethnographies and other rapid research approaches have highlighted that authors seldom report their dissemination strategies and if/how their findings were used to inform new or existing programmes or interventions, make changes in policy or practice (Johnson and Vindrola-Padros 2017; Vindrola-Padros and Vindrola-Padros 2018). In this chapter, I draw from my own experience as well as the work carried out in the field of rapid evaluation to sketch out some potential dissemination strategies that can be useful for rapid ethnographies. When referring to dissemination, researchers will often think of developing manuscripts for publication or a final report for a funder (Wilson et al. 2010a). However, this chapter uses the term 'dissemination' to refer to any type of sharing of findings (including verbal communication, short memos or reports, presentations, workshops, etc.).

Dissemination Plans

A comment I frequently hear is that when studies are rapid, it is more difficult to share findings with stakeholders on an ongoing basis. My question in these cases is: Were dissemination plans integrated in the study design? The answer is normally no. This means that issues with the ongoing sharing of findings are less the product of the short study time frames and more a result of a limited study design, one that did not take into consideration when findings would be needed and shared. When I work on study design with students or in my own research, one of the first questions we ask is: Will study findings be required at specific time points to inform decision-making? If so, who will need the findings and when? We then put together a dissemination plan based on the answers to these questions.

There is extensive literature on the development of dissemination plans, including a wide range of conceptual frameworks designed for knowledge translation. A definition of dissemination that is relevant for us is: 'a planned process that involves consideration of target audiences and the settings in which research findings are to be received and, where appropriate, communicating and interacting with wider policy and health service audiences in ways that will facilitate research uptake in decision-making processes and practice' (Wilson et al. 2010b).

I will not go over the already established conceptual frameworks for dissemination in this chapter, as these have been discussed elsewhere (Wilson et al. 2010b), but most dissemination plans consider the following factors:

1. Dissemination goals
2. Target audiences
3. Key messages
4. Sources/messengers
5. Dissemination activities, tools, timing and responsibilities
6. Budget
7. Evaluation of the impact of dissemination (Bauman et al. 2006; CHSRF 2004; ESRC 2004; Zarinpoush et al. 2007)

I have adapted these factors to the case of rapid ethnographies and ask myself the following questions when developing dissemination plans:

1. *Dissemination goals*: Are we only attempting to share knowledge/information? Do we want to use dissemination to cross-check data, gain insight and/or generate engagement?
2. *Target audiences:* Who are the relevant stakeholders and how is it best to engage them? Do these stakeholders need to change at specific time points?
3. *Key messages*: What are the main messages we need to transmit? Do we need to negotiate these in advance?
4. *Sources/messengers*: What is the best format to share these findings? Do we need to establish internal 'champions' or study 'sponsors' to disseminate the findings elsewhere?
5. *Dissemination activities, tools, timing and responsibilities*: When will findings be required? What is the best way to share these? How continuous should dissemination be? Who will have responsibility over the findings and their continuous dissemination?
6. *Budget*: How much of the funding can be used for dissemination? Who will be responsible for covering these costs? Can we think of cost-effective dissemination strategies?
7. *Evaluation of the impact of dissemination*: After dissemination, how have study findings been used? If they have not been used, why not?

The Goals of Dissemination

Some researchers have told me that they find it difficult to set up a dissemination plan when carrying out rapid ethnographies, as they want to keep their study design flexible enough to allow for some exploration and mid-study changes. A dissemination plan, however, does not mean that we need to lose the openness

Table 7.1 Example 1: Dissemination plan for a rapid ethnography of a healthcare intervention (duration: six months)

Study stage	Time into study	Type of dissemination	Purpose	Format	Type of stakeholder
Scoping/ familiarisation	Week 1	Sharing RQs and study outline	Agree purpose of the study	Face-to-face meeting	Intervention designers, implementers and users
Scoping/ familiarisation	Week 2 or 3	Sharing final study scope	Final agreement on study design and dissemination plan	E-mail or face-to-face meeting	Intervention designers, implementers and users
Fieldwork and analysis	Month 2	Short memos (monthly or weekly)	Highlight emerging findings	E-mail	Implementers
Fieldwork and analysis	Months 3–4	Short memos (monthly or weekly)	Highlight emerging findings	Face to face	Intervention designers, implementers and users
Final analysis	Month 5	Report draft	Cross-check early interpretations	E-mail or face to face	Implementers
Writing	Month 6	Final report and presentation	Final sharing of findings and development of recommendations	Face to face	Intervention designers, implementers and users

and free curiosity often associated with ethnographic research. A plan can also be flexible enough to permit serendipity in the field and a drastic change of direction. The benefits of a plan entail thinking through the potential ways in which data can be interpreted, made sense of, visualised or presented and shared, even if it is in the form of interim findings.

In Table 7.1, I have included an example of a dissemination plan we used while carrying out a rapid ethnography of a healthcare intervention over a period of six months. The study included a short scoping or familiarisation stage, which was used to define the scope of the study and agree on the format and timeline for dissemination. Findings were then disseminated and cross-checked almost on a monthly basis, either via e-mail or face to face. Table 7.2 presents a dissemination plan for a longer study (nine months) following the same principles but with a few modifications in relation to the frequency of feedback.

Thinking about the goals of dissemination early in study design also allows us to see dissemination as a process that entails more than the transfer of knowledge. The sharing of findings can actually represent a stage in the process of

Table 7.2 Example 2: Dissemination plan used during a focused ethnography of a healthcare intervention (duration: nine months)

Study stage	Time into study	Type of dissemination	Purpose	Format	Type of stakeholder
Scoping/ familiarisation	Week 1	Sharing RQs and study outline	Agree purpose of the study	Face-to-face meeting	Intervention designers, implementers and users
Scoping/ familiarisation	Week 2 or 3	Sharing final study scope	Final agreement on study design and dissemination plan	E-mail or face-to-face meeting	Intervention designers, implementers and users
Fieldwork and analysis	Month 3	Short memos (monthly)	Highlight emerging findings	E-mail	Implementers
Fieldwork and analysis	Month 5	Interim report presentation	Highlight emerging findings and cross-check early interpretations	Face to face	Intervention designers, implementers and users
Final analysis	Month 8	Final report draft	Cross-check interpretations	E-mail	Implementers
Writing	Month 9	Final report and presentation	Final sharing of findings and development of recommendations	Face to face	Intervention designers, implementers and users

knowledge co-production, where multiple stakeholders are brought together to consider the findings, cross-check interpretations or propose alternative ones (Vindrola-Padros et al. 2018). The sharing of findings early in the course of a study can also be used to secure engagement from stakeholders, as these might be more likely to be interested in a study where they can get an idea of the type of output it will produce. This early engagement should not be underestimated, as it might be required to secure access to people, areas or data necessary for the study.

The Stakeholder Group and Study Champions

In a recent commentary, I have argued in favour of including scoping studies as a stage in the design of studies (Vindrola-Padros 2020). Many researchers maintain traditional concepts of research, where the team designs a protocol, implements data collection, then conducts analysis and, ultimately, shares the findings through a final report and publications in an academic journal. Our experience in applied health research has pointed to a very important stage that is capable of shaping the entire research process, but has to happen even before the design of the final study protocol. We normally call this a 'scoping' stage, as it allows us to determine, in collaboration with all relevant stakeholders, the scope of the study. This scoping stage is an important component of the dissemination of research findings. In previous studies we have used scoping questions such as:

1. What is the programme theory underpinning the programme or service? What are the proposed benefits of change? What are the expected outcomes? Are there any potential unintended consequences or negative outcomes?
2. Who are the main stakeholders of the programme/service?
3. What are the main components of the programme/service? Which components need to be included in the evaluation?
4. Are any aspects of the service/programme already being studied?
5. What are the main costs incurred in the delivery of the programme/service? Are there any areas where you might expect cost savings?
6. How are you currently measuring the impact of the programme/service?
7. When do key decisions about the programme/service need to be made? Who will be involved in these decisions?

In a recent study on the collaboration between academic institutions and healthcare organisations, Bowen et al. (2019) found that healthcare leaders considered research to be too narrow, not applicable to the local context or answering questions that were important to them. A scoping stage carried out before the design of the study or evaluation is designed to familiarise the researcher with the context of healthcare organisations, their most pressing issues and the main priorities identified by leadership teams. The researcher might carry out some informal data collection in the form of conversations with key stakeholders, observations during meetings or events and documentary analysis. These data can then be used to inform a participatory prioritisation workshop where key stakeholders come together with the research team to discuss, and often prioritise, the areas that need to be included in the study and agree on the research questions and study design. In a recent rapid ethnography, we carried out a scoping study involving:

1. Meetings with key stakeholders (5–7 people) to obtain information on the context, current state of the programme/service and key activities (to answer the questions listed above)
2. Observations during relevant meetings
3. Review of relevant documents
4. Workshop with key stakeholders to prioritise areas for the study
5. Development of study protocol for internal approval (including draft sampling strategy for interviews, observations and documents)
6. Development of a dissemination plan for internal approval

The research team can take the data generated through these discussions and use it to draft the study protocol, which is also reviewed by the group of stakeholders. Our untested assumption is that these discussions and processes of review allow us to develop research that is more relevant to the organisations where we work. Furthermore, as areas are selected jointly and all collaborate in the design of research questions, it gives stakeholders in healthcare organisations, including leaders, a sense of ownership over the study and the findings. This stage requires time and resources, but these are outweighed by the benefits it generates in relation to the study design and the building of relationships with staff in healthcare organisations from the beginning of the study.

The group of stakeholders who are engaged from early stages needs to be selected carefully and through a process of collaboration. Anker et al. (1993) described the benefits of establishing a 'core team' of stakeholders during early stages of research to guarantee engagement and the use of findings. This group of stakeholders took responsibility over the study and participated in decisions related to design, implementation, timeline and logistics. They also facilitated access to research sites and participants to prevent delays in the implementation of the evaluation (Anker et al. 1993). Our stakeholder groups normally involve: a senior member of the organisation or design/implementation lead of the programme/service, a few people in charge of the day to day running of the programme/service, people who receive services or use the programme, people who might be involved in decision-making at a national or policy level, people who might have been against or might be skeptical in relation to the benefits of the programme/service, and external organisations or actors doing similar work or planning to do similar work in different contexts (if relevant, these can also be stakeholders working at the level of policy design).

In our experience, some of these stakeholders might then go on to play the role of 'champion' or 'sponsor' of the study, telling others about the study, providing access to people and areas for the researcher or implementing the study findings in their own work area. Initial work needs to be carried out with the group of stakeholders to outline areas of responsibility throughout the study. In the case of rapid ethnographies, we normally establish a type of written agreement indicating that the researcher will act in independent form and will share all types of findings, even those that might not be desired or might be 'uncomfortable' for some stakeholders. Some of the research we conduct might uncover aspects of a health service or programme that can affect the work carried out by stakeholders who are sitting around the table. Furthermore, we might be asked to carry out research where the findings might have negative or unintended consequences on specific groups.

It is our responsibility as researchers to maintain the independence of the study and share these findings in a constructive way. This is the reason why it is important to set out this written agreement early in the study. If issues emerge throughout the study, then researchers and stakeholders can always refer back to the agreed principles for the study. In the vignette below, I present an example of a study where this early agreement was instrumental in the survival of the study.

Vignette: Sharing uncomfortable findings

Several years ago, I was working as part of an interdisciplinary team that was asked to identify the reasons why healthcare professionals were not referring patients to a new service. The hospital had outsourced the service to a private company and needed to know the barriers to referral to negotiate a more affordable contract with the company. We carried out a rapid study to identify the main reasons for lack of referral and found out that the reasons could be grouped in the following categories: (1) increased burden (mainly administrative) created by the new service; (2) negative perception of the quality of care patients received while on the service; and (3) the fact that the new service competed with services already delivered by the hospital.

When we were approached to carry out the study, we were expected to deliver findings that could be used by the hospital to improve the service so clinicians would be motivated to refer more patients. However, we found profound issues with the service that could not be easily fixed. From the initial set-up of the service, clinicians' needs, preferences and ways of working had not been taken into consideration. The adaptation of professional cultures to the new service would probably take a long time, and might not even be fully achieved.

We, therefore, had the difficult task of communicating these findings to a group of hospital managers who were heavily invested in the success of the new service. The first thing we did was refer back to our written agreement to communicate all findings, no matter how 'uncomfortable' these might be. We presented ourselves as 'critical friends' and discussed our findings and recommendations in detail. In the end, the study was well received by managers. Each recommendation was turned into an action plan to improve the service, but eventually, the service was discontinued.

Feedback Loops or Cycles

The group of stakeholders mentioned above can also play a role outlining the time points when findings need to be shared to inform decision-making processes. Unfortunately, published examples of rapid ethnographies do not include detailed descriptions on the sharing and use of findings throughout the study. Therefore, I have relied on other approaches, such as rapid evaluations, as a way to design feedback loops or cycles to share interim findings as my ethnographies are ongoing.

Table 7.3 Examples of the steps involved in rapid feedback or rapid cycle evaluations

Rapid Feedback Evaluation (RFE)		Rapid Cycle Evaluation (RCE)	
Zakocs et al. (2015)	*McNall et al. (2004)*	*Schneeweiss et al. (2015)*	*Skillman et al. (2019)*
1. Clarify intent: Purpose, questions, study protocol	1. Collect existing data on programme performance	1. Review evaluation findings	1. Develop an analytic framework
2. Collect 'good enough' data: Collect and analyse data quickly	2. Collect new data on programme performance	2. Translate findings into actions	2. Collect data (first round)
3. Produce brief memo: Draft concise memo with main findings	3.Evaluate preliminary data	3. Make judgements based on findings	3. Analyse data and develop codebook
4. Engage in reflective debrief: Discuss findings with project team	4. Share findings/ recommendations with project team	4. Initiate implementation	4. Report findings
5. Decide if more information is needed, take action or take no action	5. Develop and analyse alternative designs for full-scale evaluation	5. Make changes in implementation (if needed)	5. Collect data (second round) adding quantitative data
Repeat feedback loops (steps 2–5)	6. Assist in developing policy and management decisions		Repeat cycle (steps 3–5)

Source: Vindrola-Padros et al. (2020).

We recently carried out a review on the use of rapid evaluations in healthcare to analyse the ways in which these evaluations were designed and implemented (Vindrola-Padros et al. 2020). We found the emergence of a type of evaluation called 'rapid feedback' or 'rapid cycle evaluations' whereby regular feedback sessions are included in the evaluation design to share findings with the implementers of interventions and programmes so changes can be made to improve them. Rapid evaluations can allow for mid-course programme corrections and allow both evaluators and implementers to adapt to changing circumstances (Skillman et al. 2019; Anker et al. 1993; Bjornson-Benson et al. 1993). Zakocs et al. (2015) also indicated that rapid evaluations, particularly RFEs, are able to facilitate communication with stakeholders, increasing buy-in into the project and creating a culture of learning. Table 7.3 includes a synthesis of the main steps used in rapid feedback and rapid cycle evaluations.

The RCE model proposed by Schneeweiss et al. (2015) began once findings were shared with decision-makers, and considered the steps involved in using the findings to inform decisions. The other three models involved earlier stages of evaluation and followed similar steps: (1) preliminary work to identify the aims, existing knowledge and design; (2) an initial data collection stage; (3) an analysis and reflection stage; (4) sharing of emerging findings with key stakeholders; (5) decisions about how to move forward (e.g. informing changes in the intervention/programme being evaluated or the data collected for the evaluation); and (6) cycle or feedback loop beginning again with another round of data collection.

In a recent study of an intervention designed to train clinicians in the use of data for quality improvement (QI), we developed feedback loops based on a timeline of when key decisions needed to be made. The first loop was set a few months after the intervention started, to provide emerging findings regarding issues with recruitment into the QI programme. The second loop was established a few months later, when decisions needed to be made about the inclusion of additional sites in the study. The third loop was set three months before the final sharing of findings, when decisions needed to be made about changing the focus of the intervention and potentially adding new activities (mainly around support for local QI).

Format of the Findings

The field of rapid evaluation has interesting examples on different ways to share findings on an ongoing basis. Bjornson-Benson et al. (1993), drawing from a rapid feedback design, developed short weekly reports to inform rapid decisions regarding the programme under evaluation, while Anker et al. (1993) developed tables with critical indicators within seven to ten days of the evaluation start date and fuller reports after several weeks. Zakocs et al. (2015) shared information in the form of a brief seven-page memo, which was distributed two weeks after data collection had ended and included information on implementation processes and recommended changes.

There has been plenty of discussion within anthropology in relation to the different ways in which we might communicate findings from ethnographic research. It is safe to say that the traditional ethnographic text, in the form of a monograph, is not the only way in which we currently share findings, as researchers have ventured to develop ethnographic films, dramatic productions (Kontos and Naglie 2006), 'ethnoarrays' (Abramson and Dohan 2015) and the use of hypermedia (Pink 2003), among others.

Collaborative approaches to ethnographic research have critiqued the authority of the ethnographer in the development of the text and have advocated in favour of the co-design of ethnographies and their co-production. In these cases, findings are also disseminated in different ways (Lassiter 2005). Approaches such as collaborative public ethnography draw from processes such as participatory action research (PAR) in the search for the plurality of perspectives and development of research that is relevant and useful for collaborators (Lassiter 2005, 2008). As Vannini and Mosher (2013) have argued, 'through the process of collaboratively conducting the research and cowriting texts, PAR bridges theory and practice through the translation of knowledge into accessible reports and pragmatic action that leads to meaningful social change.'

In the case of rapid ethnographies, we often need to appropriate a similar stance and rely on the 'translation of knowledge into accessible reports and pragmatic action' as proposed by Vannini and Mosher (2013) above. In previous rapid ethnographies, we have shared findings in the following ways:

- One-page memos developed for each week of fieldwork
- Tables summarising the key findings per site
- Recorded narratives of sites and main findings in the form of podcasts
- Animations with the main study findings (to make these accessible to a broad audience)
- Short reports (printed)
- Visual summaries and infographics
- Manuals for staff
- PowerPoint presentations
- Posters
- Leaflets
- Reports uploaded to websites
- Articles published in academic journals
- Articles published in non-academic journals
- News articles or press releases
- Book chapters
- Books

Some of the rapid ethnographies we have reviewed in this book have provided other examples of a multipronged strategy for dissemination. For instance, Armstrong and Armstrong (2018) shared findings with the care homes where they conducted their research after one week of fieldwork, providing a list of 'promising practices' for the delivery of care. The research team gave presentations at the care homes after the study ended and held workshops, seminars and other events with relevant stakeholders (Armstrong and Armstrong 2018). They also developed bookettes, that is, short and accessible paperback books with a summary of the findings. They were made available in multiple formats (print and online) and 'launched' at various public events (Baines and Gnanayutham 2018: 159).

The Use of Findings

As mentioned earlier, the existing literature on rapid ethnographies does not provide detailed descriptions of how findings can be used to make changes in practice and/or policy. When reflecting on previous studies, I have found that findings from our rapid ethnographies have been used in at least six ways:

1. *As a 'diagnostic tool' or to obtain a general understanding of a situation or context*: rapid ethnographies were a good approach to capture the different dimensions of a problem or to understand complex processes at stake.

2. *To inform the design of a service or intervention:* related to the point above about 'diagnosing' a situation, some findings have been translated into the aims or priorities for a new service or intervention.

3. *To understand the processes of delivering a service or implementing an intervention*: rapid ethnographies were able to capture the factors that played a role in the day-to-day running of a service or intervention, the problems faced by staff or users and strategies they used to overcome these.

4. *To understand the impact of delivering a service or implementing an intervention*: rapid ethnographies were able to capture participants' perceptions of impact as well as to document changes in practice.

5. *To inform changes in policies or the design of new policies*: the focus on localised contextual factors meant that rapid ethnographies could provide detailed information on the impact of policies on everyday life and the extent to which existing policies represented the lived realities of those they sought to affect. Findings from rapid ethnographies could also highlight the need for the development of new policies and the best ways to design these.

6. *To develop wider theories about why some services or interventions might or might not work*: this has normally been done by combining a series of rapid ethnographies on a specific service or intervention that have been carried out in different contexts.

Conclusion

The dissemination of study findings and their use to make changes in policy and practice remain a relatively unexplored topic in rapid ethnographies. In this chapter, I have drawn from other types of rapid approaches, such as rapid evaluations, to propose creative ways to share findings on an ongoing basis. Dissemination needs to be considered an instrumental component of the study design, and a core group of stakeholders needs to be created even before the study has started. This group can help the researcher and/or team identify the specific time points when findings need to be shared, as well as the best format. Additional work needs to be carried out to develop more dynamic processes for dissemination and evaluate the impact of rapid ethnographic research.

8 | The Future of Rapid Ethnographies

> To over-determine fieldwork practices is therefore to undermine the very strength of ethnography, the way in which it deliberately leaves openings for unanticipated discoveries and directions.
>
> (Amit 2000: 17)

There is an exciting future ahead for the development of rapid ethnographies. Our review of rapid ethnographies in healthcare pointed to an increase in the use of this label in the past ten years (Vindrola-Padros and Vindrola-Padros 2018). Since we published the review, I have seen at least a dozen new publications reporting the findings of rapid, quick, short-term or focused ethnographies. These recent publications have experimented with the rapid ethnographic approach, introducing new labels and challenges. A debate has emerged in relation to the quality of rapid ethnographies and the potential need for reporting standards or guidelines. The discussions in relation to the use of 'ethnography label' in rapid study time frames that I introduced in Chapter 2, have continued and taken on interesting forms. In this chapter, I present these new trends and set out a series of areas of development that need to be included in our future research agenda for the consolidation of the field of rapid ethnographies.

New Spin-Offs of Rapid Ethnographies

In recent years, I have seen more experimentation with the rapid ethnography label, as authors have explored different ways of carrying out research in a timely way, which often involves combining elements from different rapid research approaches. The new developments or spin-offs I have identified to date include:

- *Focused rapid ethnographic evaluation (FREE):* this is a modification of the focused ethnography approach, and it involved the extensive use of fieldnotes instead of digital recordings (Patmon et al. 2016). According to the designers of the approach, FREE was useful for analysing human–computer interactions and the assessment of emerging technologies in the workplace (Patmon et al. 2016).
- *Short-term focused video ethnographic case study*: this approach combined video footage, observational field notes, and postnatal video-cued interviews

to provide in-depth analysis of one case study or situation. Harte et al. (2016) have used it to explore the hospital design factors influencing childbirth supporters' experiences.

- *Flash ethnography*: in their study of nursing care homes, Armstrong et al. (2018) implemented 'flash ethnographies' to complement a longer study taking place in the same area. Their study was based on short fieldwork sessions lasting one week in each care home. To complement the data collection that occurred in these facilities, the research team also carried out a one-day intensive 'flash ethnography' of another care home in the same region to facilitate cross-case comparisons.

- *Rapid fieldwork approach*: following trends in human-centred computing (HCC) to optimise the design and implementation of technology, Eden et al. (2019) propose the development of a rapid fieldwork approach centred on the use of multiple focused field trips to sensitise research teams to the needs of stakeholders. Their approach is different from other ones we have discussed in this book in the sense that it was applied in 'an extreme compressed time-frame of one to two-day field trips spending between two to four hours with participants' (Eden et al. 2019: 3).

- *RAPICE*: The Rapid Assessment Procedure Informed Clinical Ethnography (RAPICE) has been recently developed in the field of clinical trials (Palinkas and Zatzick 2019) to collect and use qualitative data to understand trial implementation processes and address barriers to recruitment and other issues (see discussion in Chapter 5). It combined some of the characteristics of RAPs outlined above (i.e. multidisciplinary research teams, use of several data collection methods, iterative collection and analysis, and short study time frames) with intensive participant observation normally used in clinical ethnography (Zatzick et al. 2011). Study findings were shared regularly with the trial team to inform changes in trial delivery (Palinkas and Zatzick 2019).

- *Extreme ethnography*: this approach has been proposed by Rotman et al. (2012) as it responds to the needs of research carried out in large-scale online environments, where the field is broad and in constant transformation. The authors argue that ethnographic research needs to be adapted to meet these demands (Rotman et al. 2012).

The Need for Reporting Standards?

The development of reporting standards or guidelines in research is a contentious topic in some disciplines. This is particularly the case for qualitative research, where several authors have argued that qualitative research cannot be restricted to the reporting categories set by generic standards or assessed for quality using these criteria (Pearson et al. 2015). There is concern that reporting standards or guidelines for quality assessment will not take into consideration the diversity of qualitative research designs (Reid and Gough 2000), will be based on ill-defined criteria that are not universally agreed (Sandelowski and Leeman 2012) and will reproduce quality assessment models common in quantitative research that are not suitable for qualitative research (Yardley 2000).

Without discounting these arguments, our recent reviews of rapid qualitative research methods in health service delivery have highlighted the poor quality of reporting of study designs, lack of clarity regarding the defining characteristics of rapid research approaches, and missing information on how study findings are shared and used to make changes in practice (Johnson and Vindrola-Padros 2017; Vindrola-Padros and Vindrola-Padros 2018). We have highlighted the need to develop a framework to define and describe methodologies rigorously, and outline how findings are used (Johnson and Vindrola-Padros 2017; Vindrola-Padros and Vindrola-Padros 2018). Current debates in the use of the 'ethnography label' have also highlighted potential risks associated with rapid ethnographies, where researchers might sacrifice the use of theory for the sake of brevity, fostering an instrumental and acritical research approach (Cupit et al. 2018).

Inadequate reporting leads to incomplete descriptions of study design and implementation and an inability to assess the reliability of results and their interpretation (Moher et al. 2010). One way to improve the transparency and completeness of reporting and increase the quality of studies is through the development of reporting standards. Reporting standards can provide a framework for the review and assessment of studies and facilitate the use of findings (Moher et al. 2010). Clear reporting can also contribute to methodological innovation, as detailed information on how studies are designed and implemented is required to identify limitations and make improvements. Reporting standards have been produced for a wide range of study designs, including implementation studies (STARI) (Pinnock et al. 2017), qualitative research (COREQ) (Tong et al. 2007), observational studies (STROBE) (von Elm 2007) and quality improvement reports (SQUIRE) (Goodman et al. 2016), but there are no published standards or guidelines for rapid research. A protocol has been published for the development of guidelines for rapid reviews (PRISMA-RR), which cites the importance of clear reporting guidelines when the compilation of evidence needs to be expedited (Stevens et al. 2018).

In the conduct of rapid ethnographies, researchers encounter challenges unique to this type of short-term research that are not addressed in existing standards for qualitative or quantitative research (i.e. the need for standardised data collection tools when using teams of field researchers to save time, the pressures on sampling created by time constraints, time for reflexivity, strategies for cross-checking data, lack of consideration of the theoretical grounding of the research). In order to ensure that research is carried out rigorously despite time

Table 8.1 Utarini et al.'s (2001) eleven critical criteria for appraising RAPs

Aim: Is the aim of the study clearly described?
Subjectivity: Are the researchers' background, prior knowledge and relationship to the community and cultural competence clearly presented and addressed?
Field research guidelines: Is there an adequate description of the field guide (i.e. document outlining the approaches used in fieldwork) and rationale and process of its development?
Staff: Is the recruitment process and training of research assistants presented, and is it sound?
Data collection methods: Is the rationale for the data collection methods and types of information collected with each method clearly presented?
Selection of research sites: Is an appropriate strategy for selecting the study area(s) or research site(s) described?
Informant selection: Is a systematic process of selecting informants used and is it adequately described?
Credibility: Is a strategy for assessing the credibility of the researcher and the study established and presented?
Analysis: Is the analysis process adequately described and was it sound?
Presentation of findings: Are the findings and discussion clearly presented?
Ethics: Are ethical principles respected and is the process for informed consent described?

constraints, clear standards need to be established for the design and implementation of studies as well as for reporting of study methods and findings.

The development of these standards is an ongoing project for our team, but in the meantime we often use the eleven criteria for Rapid Assessment Procedures (RAP) proposed by Utarini et al. (2001) to improve the quality of reporting for published studies (see Table 8.1). We described RAPs in Chapter 3, where we discussed the development of rapid research approaches that acted as precursors to rapid ethnographies.

An argument can be made that the criteria set out by Utarini et al. (2001) mirrors the standards used in any qualitative or mixed-methods study (whether it is a long or short study). Our proposal for the future development of standards for rapid ethnographies could be based on the inclusion of issues or challenges that are particular to rapid research (that we have identified in our literature reviews). These include:

- Recruitment and training of local field researchers was highlighted as a potential challenge in rapid ethnographic research and a potential delay.
- Studies needed to specify if they developed adaptations of the methods to speed up data collection.
- Sampling of sites and participants was highlighted as a potential challenge in rapid research, as time pressures might mean that researchers only sample sites or participants that are more accessible (failing to capture other views or experiences).

- Key data on sample size and participant selection were missing from many studies included in the review.
- It is important for researchers to indicate if data collection methods have been adapted to suit rapid time frames.
- It was not clear if the researchers used rapid approaches to analyse and interpret the data.
- Only a few studies included information on the strategies used to disseminate the findings. The format used to share findings and the time when findings are shared influence if and how findings are used.
- Most of the studies included in our reviews did not offer a critical reflection of the research process, including how the role of the researcher shaped processes of data collection and analysis.
- Some studies included in the review did not report the length of the study.
- More reflexive approaches are required within rapid ethnographies to facilitate a more critical interpretation of the data and highlight areas of methodological improvement.
- The studies included in the review rarely reflected on the limitations of using rapid research in this context.

We have anticipated that the next steps in the development of these standards will include:

1. A consensus process to revise the draft standards: Convene a group of experts to request feedback on the existing standards and add any missing items. A draft of the current standards is included in Appendix E. The potential inclusion of quantitative approaches (for mixed-methods rapid ethnographies and rapid appraisals) will be discussed. The group of experts will also provide advice on the rapid research designs included in the standards and the potential need to differentiate between rapid appraisals and rapid ethnographies (to account for current debates on the use of 'the ethnographic label' [Cupit et al. 2018]). We anticipate that this group will include professionals with experience in rapid research, journal editors, professionals with experience in developing other reporting standards or guidelines, experts in quality improvement, patient representatives and potential users of rapid research findings (i.e. policy makers, staff from provider organisations, staff from charities or NGOs). Discussions on the standards will form part of a consensus process guided by an e-Delphi exercise (de Meyrick 2003; Hasson et al. 2000). We anticipate we will undergo two successive rounds of the exercise. The standards emerging from this consensus process will be submitted for publication in the form of a guidance statement.

2. Piloting of the standards: We will work with authors developing manuscripts on rapid studies to pilot the standards and provide feedback on their experiences of using the standards through a short survey. We will carry out interviews to assess the clarity and utility of the standards with a subgroup of the survey respondents. These interviews will allow more in-depth exploration of user experiences, gaps or difficulties encountered when using the standards and recommendations for making improvements.

3. Description and explanation of the standards: The information collected from the pilot and the interviews will be used to revise the standards, and this next iteration will be submitted for publication in the form of an explanation and elaboration document (E&E). This document will contain a detailed description of each standard and examples from published articles.

4. Review standards regularly: A plan will be developed to review the standards regularly and potentially expand them so they can be used for other rapid approaches (i.e. rapid evaluations).

The development of these future standards will generate much-needed discussions on the definition of rapid ethnographies, research quality, trade-offs in rapid research and the purpose of carrying out research in a timely manner.

The Reconfiguration of Training in Research Methods

In the book's introduction, I have discussed an increase in the use of rapid ethnographic approaches in doctoral research. Unfortunately, this does not mean that rapid research is being actively integrated into university research methods courses. The students who attend my rapid ethnography course often highlight that this is the only course on rapid research offered by the university, which limits the diversity of rapid approaches and perspectives they are exposed to. I teach an additional one-day intensive training courses for a broader audience, but students often need to pay to attend (limiting access).

Despite the long history of rapid research, it is surprising to see the lack of formal training in this field. This could due in part to the fact that rapid research approaches are often thought of as techniques one should learn 'on the go' or 'learn while doing'. While a practical element to learning is often required, lack of formal training in rapid research limits students' ability to explore the wide range of rapid research available, critically analyse the benefits and limitations of these approaches, and determine the situations when these might be appropriate. It also limits our ability to assess and improve these approaches as a collective.

In my opinion, a future trend in the development of the field of rapid ethnographies will need to be the delivery of training programmes, either as specialised courses in rapid research or integrated into more traditional research methods courses. Attendees would probably benefit from training that is practice-based, collaborative and student-led. I have included a few outlines of previous training I have delivered with these features in Appendix F. It should also maintain a critical stance, questioning the need and suitability of rapid research and outlining its challenges and limitations. A desired aim of the training would also be the fostering of creativity and innovation in research, finding new ways for the development and improvement of ethnographic research in applied settings.

Looking Ahead

The coming years will be crucial in the development of rapid ethnographies as a research field. We will need to keep track of new approaches as these emerge, mapping the broad landscape of rapid ethnography research and linking these new developments to the historical roots of rapid research we have discussed in this book. It will also be important to understand how rapid ethnographies are shaped by the context where they are implemented, as, for instance, studies taking place in the context of infectious epidemics in low- and middle-income countries (LMICs) will have different characteristics and have to overcome different challenges than those carried out in small urban schools in high-income countries (HICs). A continuous systematic review of our field as well as the delivery of training on rapid research approaches will be instrumental in these endeavors.

We will need to maintain a critical reflection on the design and implementation of rapid ethnographies, generating important discussions in relation to research quality, validity, credibility and authority. This might entail reaching consensus in relation to what we mean by 'rapid', 'ethnography' and 'high-quality' research. This might be achieved through the development of standards for reporting and quality assessment or more unstructured processes.

As we proceed with these discussions, it will be important for us to remember that ethnographic research is a changing practice, continuously adapting to the realities of our research context, trends in our disciplines and ways in which we produce knowledge. We will need to reach a balance between retaining the essence of ethnographic research, its openness as indicated by Amit (2000) in the quote above, and stretching the concept and boundaries of ethnography we have accepted and used until today. The future of rapid ethnographies lies in our willingness to create new forms of engagement, knowledge and approaches for the use of research findings to make changes in policy and practice.

Vignette: My latest rapid ethnography study during the COVID-19 pandemic

In the book's introduction, I reflect on my first attempt to carry out a rapid ethnography. It felt right to end the book with the rapid ethnography we were carrying out as I was putting the finishing touches on the manuscript. When the first cases of COVID-19 were announced in China in December 2019, we knew we would have a busy few months ahead of us. Our research team specialises in rapid research, and one of our streams of work is the generation of research evidence to inform response efforts in the context of infectious epidemics. Most of the data we generate is qualitative, which represents a different approach to other teams that normally rely on quantitative data to inform control and management strategies during epidemics.

As cases were dramatically increasing in Europe, we designed a rapid study focused on documenting the experiences of healthcare workers (HCWs) acting as front-line staff in the UK. We wanted to understand their perceptions of the virus and care delivery and document their experiences of caring for patients in this context. We knew that if we wanted to develop a study that could inform local response efforts, we would need to move quickly. Our study combined telephone interviews, observations during virtual conferences, rapid media analysis and rapid policy review. At one point, we had over twenty people working on different streams of the study. Other teams became interested in the study, and at the moment of writing this vignette, the study was being replicated in over ten countries.

The coordination of the work and quick sharing of emerging findings were only made possible thanks to all of the strategies and tools included in this book. By carrying out data collection and analysis in parallel and using the RAP sheet to summarise ongoing interview and observation findings, we were able to share emerging findings with relevant organisations almost in real time. We were also able to cross-check findings across a large group of researchers. We recorded the telephone interviews for future analysis but bypassed immediate transcription and relied on interview notes. Our ongoing conversations with the stakeholders who would be using our data meant that we could deliver relevant findings through various feedback loops and at a time when they could be used to inform decision-making (such as the opening of new temporary hospitals or the development of response management outside of London where incidence was still low). We borrowed methods from rapid evidence synthesis to carry out the rapid policy review.

Many of the researchers on the team had undergone training in rapid qualitative research with us, so they were able to train the new researchers. After a few weeks of research, we all spoke the same rapid research language and had developed a new skill-set that would certainly inform our future use of rapid ethnographies in health services research.

APPENDIX A

Annotated Bibliography of Rapid Ethnographies

Rapid Ethnographies

- Ackerman SL, Sarkar U, Tieu L, Handley MA, Schillinger D, Hahn K, et al. Meaningful use in the safety net: a rapid ethnography of patient portal implementation at five community health centers in California. *J Am Med Inform Assoc* 2017;24(5):903–912.

The study sought to understand efforts to implement portals in safety net healthcare systems that provide services for low-income populations. It took place in the US for a period of three months. The study combined in-depth interviews, focus groups, observations and a survey at four California safety net health systems and in-depth interviews at a fifth. Visits included interviews with clinicians and executives (n = 12), informal focus groups with front-line staff (n = 35), observations of patient portal sign-up procedures and clinic work, review of marketing materials and portal use data, and a brief survey (n = 45). The findings shed light on the considerable effort from the point of view of the health system to gain staff support for portal adoption and integrating portal-related work into clinic routines. However, patients faced numerous barriers to portal use. The authors found a mismatch between metrics of patient engagement and the priorities and the needs of safety net patient populations.

- Armstrong P, Lowndes R (eds). *Creative Teamwork: Developing Rapid, Site-Switching Ethnography.* Oxford University Press; 2018.

This was a team-based rapid ethnography of nursing care homes across six regions. Initial team meetings were used to prepare researchers for fieldwork. This preparation was conducted by sharing reading on methods and the research topic. Topic experts were also invited to give presentations. The team also carried out a one-day visit to a care home to get an idea of what a team-based ethnography might look like. The team reflected on what they learned, and used these findings to inform the design of the study. The team had to make difficult decisions about sampling, so some initial work was carried out with key stakeholders to find out information about potential care homes. Final decisions on sampling were informed by this feedback as well as practical issues such as transportation and level of access to sites. The study design was also informed by a short pilot study, where teams developed 'wish lists' of documents and areas to observe to see if these would be feasible to access in practice. Interview guides were also developed and tested with potential participants before formal data collection began. The team spent the initial portion of the fieldwork at each care home analysing documents on the context of the care home and carrying out interviews with managers, unions, residents' councils and family councils. This was used to obtain a deeper understanding of the particular characteristics of the care home, but it was also used to inform people about the study. These initial meetings are useful platforms to introduce the members of the research team and give key stakeholders the opportunity to ask questions about the team and the study. This particular study combined participant observation, photovoice and interviews. Interviews were carried out, and some residents were given cameras and asked to take pictures of 'good things worth sharing' (Armstrong and Armstrong 2018: 15). Data collection was carried out in pairs of researchers and these smaller teams were purposely designed to include researchers from different disciplines, gender, years of experience and country of origin. This was done to ensure different views were reflected in each of the pairs.

- Chesluk BJ, Holmboe ES. How teams work – or don't – in primary care: A field study on internal medicine practices. *Health Aff* 2010;29(5):874–879.

This rapid ethnography analysed team work dynamics in internal medicine practices in the US. The team spent five to six days in three practices, carrying out interviews and observations. They included a solo practice; a certified patient-centred medical home; and a multi-physician, multi-specialty practice connected to a local university. The study found that all three practices shared a common culture, but the practice team operated in separate social 'silos', isolating physicians from each other and from the rest of the practice staff. The authors concluded that current practice structures are mainly focused on supporting physicians' routines and had trouble accommodating the diversity of patients' needs. It will be critical to break down the silos and organise teams with shared roles and responsibilities.

- Chesluk B, Bernabeo E, Reddy S, Lynn L, Hess B, Odhner T, Holmboe E. How hospitalists work to pull healthcare teams together. *Journal of Health Organization and Management* 2015;29(7):933–947.

The study sought to document everyday practices by which hospitalist physicians negotiate barriers to effective teamwork in the US. The study lasted five months and combined observations with semi-structured interviews. The study found that hospitalists rely on inter-professional teamwork but do not support it. They face challenges trying to bridge internal hospital boundaries such as scattered patients, fragmented information, uncoordinated teams and unreliable processes. All of these factors could have an impact on the timeliness and safety of care. The authors conclude that inter-professional teamwork should be a core feature of hospital design and evaluation.

- Choy I, Kitto S, Adu-aryee N, Okrainec A. Barriers to the uptake of laparoscopic surgery in a lower-middle-income country. *Surgical Endoscopy* 2013;27(11):4009–4015.

The adoption of laparoscopy in lower-middle-income countries (LMICs) has been sporadic and minimal. The aim of this study was to analyze barriers to the adoption of laparoscopic surgery at a hospital in a LMIC. The study lasted twelve weeks, combining participant observation, semi-structured interviews and documentary analysis. The research team carried out more than 600 hours of participant observation as well as thirteen in-depth interviews and documentary analysis. In terms of findings, there were three overarching barriers identified in the study: (1) the organisational structure for funding laparoscopic procedures (where the ongoing funding structure, rather than upfront costs, of the laparoscopic program limited the number of laparoscopic cases); (2) the hierarchical nature of the local surgical culture; and (3) the expertise and skills associated with a change in practice (due to the generalist nature of surgical practice, surgeons were less willing to practice more technically complicated and time-consuming procedures). The authors conclude that these findings help identify ways to improve the adoption of laparoscopy in LMICs, while challenging economic-centric notions of the problems that affect the transfer of innovation in these settings.

- Culhane-Pera KA, Sriphetcharawut S, Thawsirichuchai R, Yangyuenkun W, Kunstadter P. Afraid of delivering at the hospital or afraid of delivering at home: A qualitative study of Thai Hmong families' decision-making about maternity services. *Maternal and Child Health Journal* 2015;19(11):2384–2392.

This rapid ethnography sought to identify Hmong families' sociocultural reasons for using and not using maternity services and suggest ways to improve service use in Thailand. It lasted six months and combined semi-structured interviews, focus groups and informal discussions. The study was based on life-history case studies of four women from each category plus their twelve husbands, and seventeen elders. The authors used grounded theory for data analysis. The study found that families disliked institutional processes that interfered with cultural birth practices, distrusted discriminatory personnel and did not like invasive, involuntary hospital procedures. When making a decision about where to deliver the baby, the families considered hospitals as a way to access care not available at home. Families also considered cost, travel distance and time as potential barriers to care. The authors argue in favour of the need to provide families with information on pregnancy risks and services available at hospitals.

- Hussain RS, McGarvey ST, Fruzzetti LM. Partition and poliomyelitis: An investigation of the polio disparity affecting Muslims during India's eradication program. *PLoS One* 2015;10(3):n/a.

The research focused on understanding the sociopolitical and historical dimensions of the polio disparity between Muslims and Hindus in India. The study lasted four months (May–August), and the team combined participant observation of vaccination teams with structured, semi-structured and unstructured interviews with 107 participants (Global Polio Eradication Initiative [GPEI] stakeholders and families with vaccine-eligible children). The study found that distrust of the government and resistance to vaccination were linked to fears of sterilisation influenced by the 'Family Planning Program' from 1976 to 1977. This situation led to environments that contributed the spread of disease, lowered vaccine efficacy and promoted the disproportionate high levels of resistance to vaccination.

- Jayawardena A, Wijayasinghe SR, Tennakoon D, Cook T, Morcuende JA. Early effects of a 'train the trainer' approach to Ponseti method dissemination: A case study of Sri Lanka. *Iowa Orthopedic Journal* 2013;33:153–160.

The Ponseti method has been established as the standard of care for the treatment of clubfoot in many developed countries due to its utility, cost-effectiveness and efficiency. The study described the successes and barriers to the Train the Trainer approach using Sri Lanka as a model country. It lasted five months and combined interviews, focus groups and direct observation with 162 patients and healthcare practitioners directly involved with clubfoot care. The study found that since the initiation of the 'train the trainer' educational program, clubfoot clinics grew from six to seven patients per week to over sixty patients per week. This growth was mainly attributed to word of mouth. The main barriers to the use of the method included: casting materials, bracing materials and a lack of a dedicated area of the clinic to conduct tenotomies under local anesthesia. Surprisingly, cost was not cited as a major barrier. The authors conclude that the method is of use in these settings, but additional research is required to explore its long-term sustainability.

- McElroy T, Konde-Lule J, Neema S, Gitta S, Uganda Sustainable Clubfoot Care. Understanding the barriers to clubfoot treatment adherence in Uganda: A rapid ethnographic study. *Disability and Rehabilitation* 2007;29 (11–12):845–855.

The rapid ethnography sought to identify barriers to adherence to the Ponseti method of clubfoot treatment in Uganda. The study was carried out by a team of researchers in eight districts, it lasted one month and combined semi-structured interviews, focus groups and observation. Interviews were carried out with parents of children with clubfoot (42), adults with clubfoot (2), community leaders (40), traditional healers (39) and practitioners treating clubfoot (38). Some forty-eight focus groups (24 male, 24 female) were carried out with general community members to identify their opinions on the potential barriers. The main barriers included: problems with resource availability and regional differences, distance to treatment site (for patients), poverty, lack of paternal support (for treatment), caregiver's other, competing, responsibilities and challenges of the treatment. The factors that acted as facilitators included: the availability of outreach and follow-up services, the establishment of counselling/caregiver-practitioner partnership, family harmony and solidarity, and receiving high-quality care. The authors conclude that the study findings can be used by health planners to develop strategies to meet the needs of patients in the effective treatment of clubfoot in Uganda.

- Schwitters A, Lederer P, Zilversmit L, Gudo PS, Ramiro I, Cumba L, et al. Barriers to health care in rural Mozambique: A rapid ethnographic assessment of planned mobile health clinics for ART. *Global Health: Science and Practice* 2015;3(1):109–116.

Mobile health clinics, implemented in 2013 in two provinces, are beginning to offer antiretroviral therapy (ART) and basic primary care services. The rapid ethnography was carried out prior to the implementation of the mobile health clinics, and it sought to identify community health practices and attitudes, including potential acceptance and use of mobile health clinics in Mozambique. The study lasted three months and combined structured and semi-structured interviews with observation in Gaza province in January 2013 and in Zambezia Province in April–May 2013 in districts where mobile health clinic implementation was planned. Interviews were conducted with 117 participants, including community leaders, healthcare providers, traditional healers, national health system patients and traditional healer patients. The main barriers to accessing health services were: transportation and distance-related issues (reliability, cost, and travel time). Community members tended to access care in both traditional and national healthcare facilities. The decision for the selection of healthcare provider depended on illness type, service distance and lack of confidence in the national health system. Participants were receptive to using mobile health clinics for their healthcare and ability to increase access to ART, but were worried of potential long waiting times due to a high level of patient demand.

- Saleem JJ, Plew WR, Speir RC, Herout J, Wilck NR, Ryan DM, et al. Understanding barriers and facilitators to the use of Clinical Information Systems for intensive care units and Anesthesia Record Keeping: A rapid ethnography. *International Journal of Medical Informatics* 2015;84(7):500–511.

The study evaluated the current use of Clinical Information Systems for intensive care units and Anesthesia Record Keeping for operating rooms and post-anesthesia care recovery settings in the US. It lasted two months and used ethnographic observations (with participant shadowing), opportunistic interviews and semi-structured interviews to explore how clinical end-users interacted with the CIS and ARK systems in the critical care and anesthesia care areas in each of three geographically distributed Veterans Affairs Medical Centers. Two observers recorded interactions and/or interview responses from eighty-eight CIS and ARK end-users. Data were coded and sorted into logical categories fieldnotes from sixty-nine shadowed participants. The study found that use of the systems was complicated due to the following factors: integration issues with other software systems; poor usability; software challenges; hardware challenges; training concerns; unclear roles and lack of coordination among stakeholders; and insufficient technical support. When sharing findings, these were organised in the following sections: interface and system-level changes that vendors or VA healthcare systems can implement; implementation factors under VA control and not under VA control; and factors that may be used to inform future application purchases.

- Ferreira S, Sayagob S, Blatc J. Going beyond telecenters to foster the digital inclusion of older people in Brazil: Lessons learned from a rapid ethnographical study. *Information Technology for Development* 2016;22(S1):26–46.

Telecenters are seen as a way to promote the inclusion of older people in Brazil in the digital landscape. The study was designed as a rapid ethnography with seventy-eight older people in a centre that teaches computer classes to seniors. The study found that the basic non-instrumental needs of older people need to be taken into consideration in order for them to obtain the necessary technological infrastructure. The study participants indicated that their main needs were coping with accessibility issues and maintaining interaction with others. The authors conclude that there is a need to develop strategies for the digital inclusion of older people in the country that go beyond the development of telecentres.

- Millen D. Rapid Ethnography: Time Deepening Strategies for HCI: Field Research. *Proceedings of the 3rd Conference on Designing Interactive Systems: Processes, Practices, Methonds, and Techniques* 2000:280–286.

This article focuses on the introduction of rapid ethnography approaches to the field of Human Computer Interaction research. The author argues that this approach can be useful for gathering user requirements, understanding and developing user models, and new product evaluation and iterative design. Rapid ethnographies respond to the demands for rapid prototyping and usability inspection techniques. According to the author, the core features of rapid ethnographies include: limiting or constraining the research focus and scope, using key informants, capturing rich field data by using multiple observers and inter-active observation techniques, and collaborative qualitative data analysis.

- Halme M, Kourula A, Lindeman S, Kallio G, Lima-Toivanen M. Sustainability innovation at the base of the pyramid through multi-sited rapid ethnography. *Corporate Social Responsibility and Environmental Management* 2016;23:113–128.

The authors suggest the integration of rapid multi-sited ethnography into Base of Pyramid (BOP) strategies to study the practices and user needs of low-income communities and develop business innovation programmes based on these needs. The multi-sited rapid ethnography was described according to the following stages: preparation, field study, data analysis and the identification of opportunity spaces. The ethnographic research was based on two- to four-week studies conducted sequentially at four sites. The study combined shadowing, photography, video recording, observations, interviews and secondary data analysis. In order to develop the guides that would be used for the interviews and observations, the team carried out a mind-mapping exercise. This exercise allowed them to create a shared understanding of the aims and scope of the research. Each site was visited by two researchers, but meetings for the entire team were planned in between each site visit to reflect on the field experience and emerging findings. Data analysis began when researchers were still in the field. Data were reviewed daily. In addition to the field notes from the interviews and observations, the researchers drafted preliminary data analysis memos (with each memo focusing on a specific topic). The process of preselecting photographs also started while researchers were still in the field, as this helped analysis when the fieldwork at all sites had ended. Data were analysed as a team using data analysis software and a pre-established data analysis framework. Data were analysed to identify opportunity spaces, that is, areas where the research data might be actionable. The study pointed to the lack of space, RE practices (repairing, reusing and recycling), developing educational materials and finding ways to give voice to the poor. The findings from the study were fed back to relevant businesses so they could inform market testing and prototyping. The insight generated from the study was generated in a way in which it could lead to actionable outcomes. An advisory board consisting of company representatives guided the study and met quarterly with the research team. A two-day innovation workshop for participating companies was organised by a con-sulting company after the end of the study. The researchers also participated company internal post-project innovation rounds.

- Mignone, J, Hiremath, G, Sabni V, Laxmi B, Halli S, O'Neil J, Rames, Blanchard J, Moses S. Use of rapid ethnographic methodology to develop a village-level rapid assessment tool predictive of HIV infection in rural India. *International Journal of Qualitative Methods* 2009;8(3):52–67.

The aim of this study was to develop a domains and indicators framework of village-level HIV/AIDS risk assessment. The authors carried out a rapid ethnography in ten rural villages of Karnataka, India. This study is used a case study to discuss similarities and differences between rapid ethnographies and rapid assessments. According to the authors, both approaches are mainly qualitative in nature, tend to be participatory and are appropriate to generate evidence for the field of public health.

- Baines D, Cunningham I. Using comparative perspective rapid ethnography in international case studies: Strengths and challenges. *Qualitative Social Work* 2011;12(1):73–88.

This rapid ethnography is based on a comparative research design to explore the challenges and strengths of rapid ethnographies. The study was based on the development of nine case studies across four countries. The research teams were composed of pairs of insider and outsider researchers. The authors conclude that rapid ethnographies are an effective way of carrying out research when a rapid turnaround of findings is required.

- Charlesworth S, Baines D. Understanding the negotiation of paid and unpaid care work in community services in cross-national perspective: The contribution of a rapid ethnographic approach. *Journal of Family Studies* 2015;21 (1):7–21.

The aim of this study was to explore how work and family are (re)configured in the workplace, mainly focusing on workers' capacity to combine paid care work and unpaid care. The study tool place in the community services sector and combined an analysis of macro and meso levels of analysis. It highlights the benefits of using a layered qualitative approach.

- Kluwin T, Morris C, Clifford J. A rapid ethnography of itinerant teachers of the deaf. *American Annals of the Deaf* 2004;149(1):62–72.

This rapid ethnography focused on exploring the experiences of itinerant teachers, that is, teachers who do not have a fixed workplace and might see multiple student of different ages in one day. The study was based on interviews with ten itinerant teachers in two school districts and an additional twenty-one interviews with staff who worked with itinerant teachers. The study also relied on the use of participant observation and the analysis of archival data. The study found that itinerant teachers were able to create a positive depiction of their role based on specific personality traits, long-term experience and specific value systems.

- Mudiyanselage N. 'Rapid' but not 'raid': A reflection on the use of rapid ethnography in entrepreneurship research. *Qualitative Research Journal* 2017;17(4):254–264.

This article explores the use of rapid ethnography in the context of business decision-making processes for micro-entrepreneurs. According to the authors, rapid ethnographies that use collaboration, field guides and clear schedules are able to assist with preparation, planning, technology-assisted techniques and non-traditional socialisation processes.

- McKeown M, Thomson G, Scholes A, Edgar F, Downe S, Price O, Baker J, Greenwood P, Whittington R, Duxbury J. Restraint minimisation in mental health care: legitimate or illegitimate force? An ethnographic study. *Sociology of Health and Illness* 2020;42:449–464.

This study explores the role of physical restraint practices in the context of mental health service delivery. A rapid ethnography approach was developed to look at the organisational culture and behaviour of clinical teams in 14 acute admission mental health wards in the North West of the English NHS and explore the implementation of the REsTRAIN Yourself' (RYS) initiative. The study found that the daily life on the wards before and after the implementation of the initiative was shaped by legitimation, meaningful activity, and therapeutic engagement. The authors highlighted the need to take into consideration the observed materialities of routine care.

- Brown-Johnson C, Shaw J, Safaeinilli N, Chan G, Mahoney M, Asch S, Winget M. Role definition is key – Rapid qualitative ethnography findings from a team-based primary care transformation. *Learning Health Systems* 2019.

The aim of the study was to explore the processes of implementing team-based care in primary care settings. The study used a rapid ethnography design including seventy-four hours of observation and twenty-eight semi-structured interviews. The study found that the different stakeholders had positive perceptions of care. Care coordinators were able to effectively manage care between visits. The fact that specialist care was co-located facilitated patient access to supported diabetes services and mental healthcare. The authors concluded that the rapid ethnography was useful for providing rapid and actionable findings to shape these roles so they can adapt to patients' needs.

Quick Ethnographies

- Mullaney T, Pettersson H, Nyholm T, Stolterman E. Thinking beyond the cure: A case for human-centered design in cancer care. *International Journal of Design* 2012;6(3):n/a.

The study aimed to explore the experiences of patients undergoing radiotherapy treatment. Drawing from work in the field of patient-centred care, the study used a human-centered design research approach to identify aspects of care that triggered patient anxiety. The study was designed as a quick ethnography following Handwerker's (2001) proposal. According to the authors, a quick ethnography design 'enables researchers to gather rich data without direct interaction with the object of study' (Mullaney et al. 2012). The authors combined patient observations, informal interviews with staff, photographic documentation and self-reported materials with patients to collect data on patient interactions and patients' emotional responses to these. The first phase of the study (two weeks) relied on the use of observational methods to map out the patient journeys in the hospital, while the second phase was used to explore patient experience. The study involved observations with thirty members of staff from different professional groups and twelve informal interviews to do the mapping described in phase 1 and observations with sixty-two patients for the second phase. The authors also asked fourteen patients to record their experiences through the use of photo cameras and diaries to document their experiences during five weeks of treatment. The authors drew from frameworks used in the field of Science and Technology Studies (STS) to analyse the data. One of the main findings from the study was that fixation technology used in radiotherapy was a key trigger of anxiety in patients. These types of devices depict the patient as passive and disempowered in their 'sick role'. The authors suggest the use of design to change social perceptions of the role of the patient to powerful users within the healthcare system.

Focused Ethnographies

- Dupuis-Blanchard S, Neufeld A, Strang VT. The significance of social engagement in relocated older adults. *Qualitative Health Research* 2009;19(9):1186–1195.

Relocation is a common aspect of the lives of many seniors and it is often associated with the disruption of social networks. The aim of the study was to identify the meaning of social engagement for adults who had recently moved to flats for older people and the types of relationships they developed in their new homes. The study used semi-structured interviews with nineteen older adults and an ecomap consisting of a central circle, to represent the participant, with outer circles representing other significant people. The interview transcripts were analysed using thematic analysis. The study found that seniors developed four types of relationships: for provision of feelings of security, casual interactions, supportive relationships and friendships.

- Ensign J, Bell M. Illness experiences of homeless youth. *Qualitative Health Research* 2004;14(9):1239–1254.

The focused ethnography sought to describe the experiences of homeless youths of illness and how these experiences differed by age, gender and sampling site. The researchers carried out participant observation in the youth clinic and street areas, key informant interviews, semi-structured interviews in a private consulting room in the clinic or street-side in the front seats of the medical van, focus group interviews for more in-depth exploration of identified themes and topics. A total of forty-five young people aged fifteen to twenty-three years took part in the study. The study found that underage youth were denied medical attention, and those above the age of eighteen cited inability to cover healthcare bills as a barrier. Young people living on the street reported a higher level of disease and substance abuse and tended to rely on the use of emergency services.

- Garcia C, Saewyc E. Perceptions of mental health among recently immigrated Mexican adolescents. *Issues in Mental Health Nursing* 2007;28(1):37–54.

The study sought to explore the health-related perceptions and experiences of immigrant Latino adolescents. The research team collected information from two interviews and pictures taken by fourteen participants, who had been given twenty-four-exposure disposable cameras. They also carried out participant observation. The authors identified three main themes: mentally healthy, mentally unhealthy and health promotion. The authors conclude that there is a need for increased awareness of the impact of immigration on the mental health needs of Latinos and the role mental health nurses need to play to influence access to medical services.

- Higginbottom GMA. The transitioning experiences of internationally-educated nurses into a Canadian health care system: a focused ethnography. *BMC Nursing* 2011;10(14):1–13.

The study sought to understand internationally educated nurses' (IENs) transitioning experiences on relocation to Canada. The focused ethnography involved thirty-one semi-structured interviews with twenty-three IENs at one to three months post relocation and nine to twelve months post relocation. The sample was purposive and included nurses educated to first degree and higher and most employed as 'graduate nurses'. Data analysis was informed by Roper and Shapira's framework for focused ethnography. The study found that many IENs had negative work experiences related to their job plans and the lack of support provided by their workplace. The author concludes that there is a need for the improvement of communication channels between nurses and their employers and the development of pre-arrival orientation and inductions upon arrival to make sure IENs have all of the relevant information and the opportunity to voice concerns.

- Kilian C, Salmoni A, Ward-Griffin C, et al. Perceiving falls within a family context: A focused ethnographic approach. *Canadian Journal on Aging* 2008;27(4):331–345.

The authors sought to examine the perceptions of risk regarding falling older adults and their adult children, and what personal, interpersonal and societal factors influence these perceptions. The study was designed as a focused ethnography, it took place in Canada and combined semi-structured interviews with observation. Thematic analysis was conducted to identify themes within groups and to compare the perspectives of older adults and adult children. The study found that there were differences in perceptions and approaches to action between older adults and their adult children. In addition to parents' actions and shared actions, the authors found that children also carried out secret actions with the aim of preventing injuries in the older adults. The authors concluded that a combination of approaches is necessary to guarantee the well-being of older adults, and this should entail recognition of the independence of older adults as well as the perceptions of other family members (i.e. their children) on how to prevent injuries.

- Patmon F, Gee P, Rylee T, Readdy N. Using interactive patient engagement technology in clinical practice: A qualitative assessment of nurses' perceptions. *Journal of Medical Internet Research* 2016;18(11):30–42.

Patient engagement technology systems, also referred to as interactive patient engagement technologies (iPET), are often identified as an effective way to promote patient engagement. The aim of this study was to examine nurses' perceptions of patient engagement technology systems and identify barriers and promoting factors that affect utilisation. The team used participant observation in two California-based hospitals and semi-structured interviews with thirty-eight nurses. Data were recorded in the form of fieldnotes. After each day of data collection, the researchers reviewed the fieldnotes to identify emerging findings and areas that required further exploration. Coding was carried out by using a codebook and data analysis software. The analysis process involved other members of the research team to cross-check coding and the development of themes. The authors also went through a process of member checking. Throughout the study, the researchers engaged in a critical reflection of their work, documenting preconceptions and doubts. The study found that iPETs were effective for distraction therapy, had functionality that affects both patients and nurses, had implications for clinical practice and may require additional training to improve use. The authors concluded that the improvement of training on the iPET system could lead to the enhancement of nursing practice. The systems also acted as a distraction for patients. Findings were shared once the analysis was complete. The findings were shared with key stakeholders (manly managers and senior nursing staff members).

- Pasco AC, Morse JM, Olson JK. The cross-cultural relationships between nurses and Filipino Canadian patients. *Journal of Nursing Scholarship* 2004;36(3):239–246.

The focused ethnography sought to identify the culturally embedded values that implicitly guide Filipino Canadian patients' interactions in developing nurse-patient relationships. The research team carried out face-to-face unstructured interviews with twenty-three Filipino Canadians who received care in Canadian hospitals initiated with a 'grand tour' question and observations. The study found that patients shaped the care experience by using cultural beliefs to determine their preference for who performed personal and private tasks while seeking care and who could receive information. Some of the reasons why patients could not progress through all desired cultural levels were: the urgency of the patient's condition, the intimacy required for most nursing procedures and the short period of hospitalisation. The authors conclude for the need to develop culturally safe nurse–patient relationships.

- Scott SD, Pollock C. The role of nursing unit culture in shaping research utilization behaviors. *Research in Nursing and Health* 2008;31(4):298–309.

The purpose of the study was to explore the effect of unit culture on the general use of research by nurses in a paediatric critical care unit. The focused ethnography combined individual interviews with observations. The study found that the aspects of the unit's culture that shaped nurses' research utilisation were: a hierarchical structure of authority, routinised and technology-driven work at the bedside, ethos that discouraged innovation, and emphasis on clinical experience. Nurses were reluctant to envision other ways of working and integrating research into routine practice.

- Spiers JA, Wood A. Building a therapeutic alliance in brief therapy: The experience of community mental health nurses. *Archives of Psychiatric Nursing* 2010;24(6):373–386.

The study sought to explore perceptions and actions of community mental health nurses in building a therapeutic alliance in the context of brief therapy and the factors that helped or impeded its development. The research team carried out three focus groups and individual interviews with eleven nurses who had at least three years of experience in community mental health. The study found that the therapeutic alliance was created through three main phases: establishing mutuality, finding reciprocal exchange and activating the power of the client.

- Tzeng WC, Yang CI, Tzeng NS, et al. The inner door: Toward an understanding of suicidal patients. *Journal of Clinical Nursing* 2010;19(9–10):1396–1404.

The focused ethnography described the ways psychiatric nurses provided care, and responded to dilemmas associated with caring, for suicidal patients. The study combined participant observations and eighteen interviews with psychiatric nurses in a medical centre in Taipei, Taiwan. The study found that nurses developed an inner understanding of the worlds of suicidal patients, and when this understanding was missing, they labelled the patients and even restrained them. The authors conclude that additional work is required by nurses to resolve their own inner conflicts so they are able to appreciate the experiences of their patient and provide better care.

- Kitchen CEW, Lewis S, Tiffin PA, Welsh PR, Howey L, Ekers D. A focused ethnography of a Child and Adolescent Mental Health Service: Factors relevant to the implementation of a depression trial. *Trials* 2017;18:237.

A focused ethnography was carried out prior to a randomised controlled trial to ensure the setting was adequate for the trial. The study combined 158 hours of observation, 6 formal interviews with staff and the analysis of 17 documents. Data were analysed using thematic analysis. The study found that staff decisions were sometimes based on non-clinical factors such as resource availability. Staff experienced different levels of confidence in relation to making patient diagnoses. Staff capacity were shaped by their ability to attend training and capacity to integrate learning into practice. The study findings were integrated into the trial protocol.

- Smallwood, A. Cardiac assessment teams: A focused ethnography of nurses' roles. *British Journal of Cardiac Nursing* 2009;4(3):132–139.

A cardiac assessment team needed to be developed to assist in the management of acute coronary syndrome patients. The aim of this focused ethnography was to explore the roles of nurses working in two settings: a medical assessment unit and the emergency department. The study design included interviews with staff and participant observation in these two settings. The study found that the cardiac assessment team had four main roles: gatekeeper, specialist consultancy practice, catalyst and diplomat. These roles changed depending on the organisational culture.

- Bikker A, Atherton H, Brant H, Porqueddu T, Campbell J, Gibson A, McKinstry B, Salisbury C, Ziebland S. Conducting a team-based multi-sited focused ethnography in primary care. *BMC Medical Research Methodology* 2017;17:139.

The authors implemented a team-based approach to focused ethnography in the context of health services research. According to these authors, health services research, with a multi-sited study design, many times requires the use of teams of researchers to cover and exert responsibility over particular sites (Bikker et al. 2017). Furthermore, health services research also requires the combination of a wide range of expertise, a need that is addressed with the creation of multidisciplinary teams of researchers (Bikker et al. 2017). The first step the authors took, even before study design, was the development of a conceptual review which would be used to inform the FE design as well as the study materials (i.e. observations, interviews and coding framework). The findings from the review were also used to inform the sampling and develop a guidance document for the field researchers. The research reported by Bikker et al. (2017) was spread over eight primary care practices in three different geographic locations. The authors combined non-participant observations of the practices, informal conversations with staff, semi-structured interviews with staff and patients, and document review (minutes of meetings and relevant practice protocols). The FE team was made up of three field researchers recruited for the purpose of the study and two researchers who led and supervised this work. The field researchers divided up the fieldwork across the eight sites. The team had a workshop before data collection began, to familiarise themselves with the study design and with each other. The team also went through a training exercise during the workshop where they all observed the same setting, compared styles of observation and developed a shared approach. The authors use a study developed in primary care in the UK as a case study to discuss this approach.

- Mason B, Epiphaniou E, Nanton V, Donaldson A, Shipman C, Daveson BA, Harding R, Higginson I, Munday D, Barclay S, Boyd K, Dale J, Kendall M, Worth A, Murray SA. Coordination of care for individuals with advanced progressive conditions: A multi-site ethnographic and serial interview study. *British Journal of General Practice* 2013:e580–e588.

The aim of this study was to identify how care is coordinated in generalist settings for individuals with advanced progressive conditions during the last year of life. The focused ethnography combined serial interviews with fifty-six patients, twenty-five of their family carers and seventeen healthcare workers. The study lasted twenty-two weeks and was carried out in a regional hospital, a large general practice and a respiratory outpatient service. The study found that a small number of patients had been identified for palliative care. The main factors limiting the identification of palliative care needs included rapid throughput of hospital patients and time pressures in primary care. The authors also found lack of care coordination when patients were admitted through the emergency department or when they were discharged from hospital. The authors conclude with the need to develop a model to improve the coordination of care for patients during the end of life so they can be identified in a timely manner.

- Skårås M. Focused ethnographic research on teaching and learning in conflict zones: History education in South Sudan. *Forum for Development Studies* 2018;45:2:217–238.

The purpose of this article is to discuss the benefits of using focused ethnography to produce knowledge on teaching and learning in conflict zones. The author argues that methods such as video observation, 'hanging out' and interviews are good methods to collect data in settings experiencing violence. The article draws on a case study of education in South Sudan to demonstrate how contexts shaped by conflict require particular approaches to research. According to the author, researchers working in these settings need to consider potential challenges of restricted access, psychological stress, complexity, positionality of the researcher and unpredictability. A focused ethnography approach allows for in-depth analysis and triangulation of data over a short period of time.

- Andreassen P, Christensen M, Møller J. Focused ethnography as an approach in medical education research. *Medical Education* 2019; https://doi.org/10.1111/medu.14045

This article discusses the benefits of using focused ethnographies in medical education research. Focused ethnographies are able to cover short-term episodes not bound to single sites and can capture a diverse and multifaceted field.

- Conte KP, Shahid A, Grøn S, et al. Capturing implementation knowledge: applying focused ethnography to study how implementers generate and manage knowledge in the scale-up of obesity prevention programs. *Implementation Science* 2019;14:91. https://doi.org/10.1186/s13012-019-0938-7.

The aim of this study was to evaluate two evidence-based childhood obesity prevention programs. The focused ethnography lasted twelve months and included a multi-sited ethnography of fourteen implementation teams. The study found that the teams used tools to manage and store information for implementation. These tools had the following functions: (1) relationship management, (2) monitoring progress towards target achievement, (3) guiding and troubleshooting PHIMS use, (4) supporting teamwork, (5) evaluation, and (6) recording extra work at sites not related to program implementation. The study also highlighted the importance of tacit knowledge about implementation.

- Plaza del Pino FJ, Soriano E, Higginbottom GM. Sociocultural and linguistic boundaries influencing intercultural communication between nurses and Moroccan patients in southern Spain: A focused ethnography. *BMC Nursing* 2013;12:14.

The aim of this focused ethnography was to identify how nurses perceive their intercultural communication with Moroccan patients and the barriers that might prevent communication and care. The study combined semi-structured interviews with thirty-two nurses in three hospitals in Spain. The study found that one of the main barriers between nurses and patients was language, followed by prejudices and social stereotypes. The authors conclude that additional training on culturally appropriate and sensitive care is required for nurses in Spain.

- Gagnon AJ, Carnevale F, Mehta P, et al. Developing population interventions with migrant women for maternal-child health: A focused ethnography. *BMC Public Health* 2013;13:471.

The aim of this focused ethnography was to explore the concerns of migrant women in relation to their children's health during early months and years. The study was based on in-depth interviews with sixteen women and participant observation. The study found that women used a wide range of coping strategies to respond to their concerns. Social inclusion was associated with resiliency. The study documented a series of recommendations made by participants for the development of programmes.

Short-Term Ethnographies

- Harte JD, Sheehan A, Stewart SC, Foureur M. Childbirth supporters' experiences in a built hospital birth environment. *Health Environments Research & Design Journal* 2016;9(3):135–161.

The study focused on identifying the design factors that inhibited or facilitated the practices of childbirth supporters in a hospital in Australia. The authors carried out a short-term focused video ethnographic single case study of the birthing experiences of one family. The researcher combined video recording of the birth, video-cued interviews with the family and birth supporters, interviews with midwives and observations of the built environment. The data were analysed using thematic analysis. The researcher analysed text as well as video data through three analysis cycles. The process of watching the video during the video-cued interviews served as a data-gathering technique as well as a member-checking process. The experiences of birth supporters were complex and complicated by their limited understanding of the environment and by other staff members' willingness to adapt the setting to their needs. Their role was strained between feelings of being needed and being 'in the way'.

APPENDIX B

Field Guides (Examples)

RREAL Tool for Rapid Anthropological Assessments in the Field (Context Humanitarian Crises)

Our lab has developed a rapid anthropological assessment tool for the Office of US Foreign Disaster Assistance (Johnson et al. 2019). Rapid anthropological assessments should begin with the creation of an initial local data profile using available data. This data can then be supplemented (as needed) using the following types of rapid anthropological assessments: contextual assessment, risk and health consequences assessment, and intervention assessment (Stimson et al. 1999; Trotter et al. 2000).

The table below provides a model, suggested methodology and questions to use for rapid anthropological assessments. This data has been adapted from prior rapid anthropological assessments (Agyepong et al. 1994; Stimson et al. 1999; Trotter et al. 2000) supplemented with the authors experiences in the field. These should be used as *guiding questions* for data collectors to use responsively to context and need. Data collection activities should prioritise addressing existing evidence gaps with subsequent analysis focused upon collecting data to aid responders.

Contextual assessments

Aim: Document social and environmental conditions – time, place and sociocultural processes which contribute to risk and protective factors for disease transmission – faced by at-risk populations. Ask *where*, *why* and *how* people do things which contribute to resilience and vulnerability and either facilitate or impede participation in interventions.

Expected outcome: To develop effective, locally relevant interventions for prevention and care. Collect available data which is highly contextualized to the affected population and the priorities of public health responders. A primary purpose in a contextual assessment is to *identify information gaps* to be addressed by the rapid anthropological assessment.

Factors that facilitate or discourage the spread of _____ .
- Are there particular social groups who are vulnerable to [X]?
- Are there any racial, ethnic or other divisions in society which have an impact on [X]?
- Are particular social roles disproportionally affected by [X]? How does gender and age shape this?

(cont.)

- What is the effect of any laws/policies regarding [X]? How are the laws implemented?
- Are there features of the geographical environment that facilitate/constrain the spread of [X]?
- Are there significant movements of population (e.g. migration, economic) relevant to the spread of [X]?
- What economic features are important to understanding the spread of [X] (e.g. mobility, income inequality)?
- What features of the political environment might contribute to the spread of [X] (e.g. rapid political change)?

Factors that increase or decrease health and social consequences of _____.
- Are local healthcare systems able to provide care and treatment for people with [X]?
- How do different healthcare providers (biomedical and alternative) frame [X] in their diagnosis and treatment?
- What aspects of the role of men, women and children affect the risks and consequences of [X]?
- What aspects of age affect the risks and consequences of [X]?
- What are the key health problems of affected populations which have an impact on [X]?
- Are there local social welfare systems able to help people with [X]?
- What views are held about [X] by different sectors of the population (e.g. government officials, religious leaders)?
- Who does the population consider a trustworthy source of health-related information?
- Do households and families support/believe or reject/disbelieve biomedical understanding of [X] risks?
- Are there other explanations offered for the spread, risks and consequences of [X]?

Factors that hinder or enable interventions to control spread of _____.
- What health services and health workers are available and accessible (e.g. government provided, informal)?
- Are there local influential groups that affect the implementation of interventions?
- Are there community-based organisations (CBO) which operate in the field of [X] or in related fields?
- Is there local capacity for research and evaluation on [X]?
- How influential are religious groups? What are their views on [X]? Other local influential groups?
- Are there any racial, ethnic, language or other divisions that help or hinder the development of interventions?
- What sources of media are accessible to and trusted by the population? Who controls/influences these sources?

Risk and health consequence assessments
Aim: Document the **type**, **extent** and **nature** of risks encountered by high-risk populations. Data should complement contextual data (where relevant) in assessing why people engage in risk behaviour and the social factors that facilitate or impede risk reduction.
Expected outcome: To draw out key findings to be included in an action plan.

Individual risk behaviours – *Assessment questions should focus on factors that lead to risk; knowledge, values, beliefs, etc. which may cause persons to engage in risk behaviour; and protective factors which reduce risk.*

(cont.)

- What individual behaviours increase the risk of adverse health consequences? What is the extent and frequency of risk?
- What are individual levels of knowledge and their perceptions of the risks associated with [X] transmission?
- Why do individuals engage in risk behaviours (knowledge, values, beliefs) if knowing their behaviour may cause the potential for harm?
- How can risks be avoided or reduced?

Community risk factors – *Assessment questions should focus of risk behaviours which are influenced by wider peer, family, community and social groups regarding what is considered normal/acceptable/appropriate behaviour.*

- How do social norms and practices influence risk behaviour?
- How does the social settings influence risk behaviour?
- Do particular groups have higher levels of risk behaviour? Why?

Structural factors – *Assessment questions should focus on how policy, law, environment etc. influence risk behaviour at the community level.*

- What impact do local and national policies have on community risk behaviour?
- What impact does the social, economic and legal environment have on community risk behaviour?

Effective and sustainable risk reduction interventions often require changes at all three levels of analysis (i.e. individual, community and structural changes).

Intervention assessments

Aim: Determine the positive and negative benefits of current, planned for or potential public health interventions. Where no interventions exist, assessments may serve to identify their need and/or outline a protocol for interventions to reduce risk and increase/reinforce community resilience mechanisms.

Expected outcome: To draw out key findings to be included in an action plan.

Who is reached by what interventions, and with what effect?

Current/existing interventions

- What are the current local interventions targeting [X] risks and consequences?
- What is the adequacy and effectiveness of current interventions? How is success measured by different populations?
- Who should be involved in the response according to the communities? Who is deemed trustworthy?

New or expanded interventions

- What interventions are needed that do not currently exist? What actors should be involved?
- What interventions need to be expanded?

Source: Johnson et al. (2019)

Credits

This rapid anthropological assessment tool has been drafted by Dr. Ginger A. Johnson and Dr. Cecilia Vindrola-Padros, Co-Directors of Rapid Research Evaluation and Appraisal

Lab (RREAL). Significant input on content was added by RREAL members Silvie Cooper and Nehla Djellouli, with designs by Angie McAfee. We would like to thank Dr. Linda Whiteford (University of South Florida), Santiago Ripoll (IDS) and Ingrid Gercama (Anthrologica) for their review and input into earlier drafts of this document.

Key Readings

Since at least the 1980s, anthropologists have developed and used rapid anthropological procedures (RAPs); rapid ethnographic assessments (REAs); rapid appraisals and qualitative inquiries; rapid assessment, response and evaluations (RARE); and 'quick ethnographies' to help social scientists and non-social scientists alike collect data to inform health program planning and implementation. See: [1] Scrimshaw SC, Hurtado E. Anthropological involvement in the Central American diarrheal disease control project. *Social Science & Medicine* 1988;27:97–105. [2] Bentley M, Pelto G, Straus W, Schumann D, et al. Rapid ethnographic assessment: Applications in diarrhea management program. *Social Science and Medicine* 1988;27 (1):107–116. [3] Agyepong IA, Aryee B, Dzikunu H, Manderson L. *The Malaria Manual: Guidelines for the Rapid Assessment of Social, Economic and Cultural Aspects of Malaria.* Geneva: United Nations Development Programme, World Bank, World Health Organization Special Program for Research and Training in Tropical Disesase (TDR); 1995. [4] Beebe J. Basic concepts and techniques of rapid appraisal. *Human Organization* 1995;54(1):42–51. [5] Brown D, Hernández A, Saint-Jean G, Evans S, et al. A participatory action research pilot study of urban health disparities using rapid assessment response and evaluation. *American Journal of Public Health* 2008;98: 28–38. [6] Stimson GV, Fitch C, Rhodes T, Ball A. Rapid assessment and response: Methods for developing public health responses to drug problems. *Drug and Alcohol Review* 1999;18(3):317–325. [7] Trotter RT, Needle RH. *RARE Project: Field Assessment Training Methods Workbook.* Washington, DC: Department of Health and Human Services; 2000.

Example of field guide developed by Bentley et al. (1988) to explore dietary management of diarrhoea in Peru.

I. Introduction
a. purpose of the project
b. purpose of the use of ethnographic guide
c. field ethics and interview methods
II. Background site information
a. collection of secondary data
b. description of ecological, socio-cultural, political site
c. food production, availability, preparation

(cont.)

d. Women's work roles and time allocation
III. Selection of field sites and informants
a. rough demographic mapping
b. identification of key informants
c. identification of non-key informants
IV. Illness taxonomies
a. illnesses commonly experienced: names, symptoms, causes, consequences
b. child illnesses: names, symptoms, causes, consequences
c. diarrhoea: how does it fit into larger illness taxonomy
V. Diarrhoea-building a 'folk taxonomy' of diarrhoea
a. general beliefs about diarrhoea
b. names of each diarrhoea type
c. definitions, symptoms, causes, consequences and treatments of each diarrhoea type
d. developmental sequence of episode by diarrhoea 'type'
VI. Child feeding
a. normal feeding patterns
1. beliefs about child feeding
2. weaning foods
a. age of introduction
b. preparation
b. feeding during/after diarrhoea
1. general beliefs about feeding during diarrhoea
2. foods to be avoided (list, reasons)
3. 'special' foods to be given (list, reasons)
4. variation by diarrhoea 'type'
5. variations in feeding during stages of illness, convalescence
VII. 'The last diarrhoea episode'
a. description of episode: when, who, why (perceived cause), symptoms, treatments given, feeding during diarrhoea, outcome of episode
VIII. Analysis of data and report writing

List of topics and methods covered in the RAP manual data collection guides developed by Scrimshaw and Hurtado (1987)

Area	Method	Description
Community		
C. 1 Geographic characteristics	Documentary analysis, observations	
C.2 Demographic and epidemiologic characteristics	Documentary analysis, interviews, observations	

(cont.)

Area	Method	Description
C.3 Socio-economic characteristics	Documentary analysis, interviews, observations	
C.4 Overview of health resources	Interviews, observations	
Household		
H. 1 Household composition	Interviews	
H. 2 Household conditions	Interviews, observations	
H. 3 Socio-economic status	Interviews, informal conversations	Employment, land owned/rented, land cultivated, food stored, food sold, dependents.
H. 4 Definitions of health and illness	Interviews, informal conversations	
H. 5 Common illnesses in children and possible treatments	Interviews, informal conversations, observations	Knowledge of illness, gravity, remedies or treatments, expenses, prevention.
H. 6 Foods eaten by mothers and children	Interviews, observations	
H. 7 Diet and sick children	Interviews, informal conversations and observations	
H. 8 Morbidity history of adult family members	Interviews	List of illnesses in the past two weeks.
H. 9 Morbidity history of children five years of age and under	Interviews	List of illnesses in the past two weeks and during the course of the study.
H. 10 Inventory of household remedies	Interviews, observations	Use, origin, cost and purpose.
H. 11 History of most recent pregnancies and deliveries	Interviews	
H. 12 Use of health resources	Interviews	
H. 13 Use and experiences with official health resources	Interview/informal conversations	
Primary healthcare providers		
P. 1 Interview with head of community health service	Interview	Schedule, services offered, personnel, equipment, cost of services and

(cont.)

Area	Method	Description
		medicines to patients, methods of payment, utilization.
P. 2 Interview with health staff	Interview	Interview with each staff member in the community health service.
P. 3 Physical characteristics of health resource	Observation	Make a map and draw the route the patient follows. Describe the environment, including any visual or educational aids.
P. 4 The waiting room	Observation	Number of patients waiting and under what conditions, length of time they wait, activities that take place while patients wait, interaction between staff and patients, positive and negative aspects of the environment.
P. 5 The consultation	Observation	Sequence of events, interactions, explanation and instructions given to the patient.
P. 6 Food distribution and/or anthropometric examination	Observation	Describe the complimentary food distribution programme and the anthropometric assessment.
P. 7 Summary of user visit to health resource	Observation	Summarize the user's visit to the health resource by recording information in a table.
P. 8 Pharmacies and stores selling pharmacies	Interview	Interview the owner or manager at each pharmacy store.
P. 9 Pharmacy staff	Interview	Interview staff members at stores that sell medicines.
P. 10 Exit interview	Interview	Interview patients as they leave the health resource.
P. 11 Knowledge of diarrhoea and oral rehydration	Interview	Interview each staff member charged with the duties of primary care.
P. 12 Preparation of oral solution	Observation	If there are packets of oral rehydration salts, observe the preparation of the solutions.
P. 13 Growth monitoring and immunization	Interview	Interview each staff member responsible for growth monitoring and/or immunization.
P. 14 Provider–patient interaction	Observation	

APPENDIX C

Generic Protocol for Rapid Literature Reviews Used to Inform the Design of Rapid Ethnographies

We will conduct a rapid literature review following the rapid review method proposed by Tricco et al. (2017). The rapid review method follows a systematic review approach but proposes adaptations to some of the steps to reduce the amount of time required to carry out the review, i.e. the use of large teams to review abstracts and full texts, and extract data; in lieu of dual screening and selection, a percentage of excluded articles is reviewed by a second reviewer, and software is used for data extraction and synthesis, as appropriate (Tricco et al. 2017).

We will use the Preferred Reporting Items for Systematic Reviews and Meta-Analysis (PRISMA) statement (Moher et al. 2009) to guide the reporting of the methods and findings. The review protocol will be registered with PROSPERO.

Review Research Questions

The review will seek to answer the following questions [list questions].

Search Strategy

We will use a staged search approach (Tricco et al. 2017). The first stage will be broad. The second stage will be targeted. We will conduct a review of published literature using multiple databases: MEDLINE, CINAHL PLUS, PsychInfo, EMBASE and Web of Science [these can change depending on the review topic]. Results will be combined into Mendeley and duplicates removed. The reference lists of included articles will be screened to identify additional relevant publications. We will search for relevant grey literature using Open Grey and TRIP.

Selection

Following rapid review methodology (Tricco et al. 2017), one researcher will screen the articles in the title phase, and three researchers will cross-check exclusions in the abstract and full-text phases. Disagreements will be discussed until consensus is reached, and an additional reviewer might be added to facilitate this process. The inclusion criteria used for study selection will be: [list criteria, pay attention to ways to limit the search by language, date of publication, geographical area, etc. to make it manageable over a short period of time].

Data Extraction and Management

The included articles will be analysed using a data extraction form developed in REDCap (Research Electronic Data Capture). The form will be developed after the initial screening of full-text articles. It will then be piloted independently by two researchers using a random sample of five articles. Disagreements will be discussed until consensus is reached. The data extraction form will be finalised based on the findings from the pilot. Two reviewers will divide up the articles and extract data simultaneously.

Data Synthesis

Data will be exported from REDCap and the main article characteristics will be synthesised. The REDCap summary report will be used to facilitate this process. The information entered in free text boxes will be exported from REDCap to an Excel spreadsheet and analysed using framework analysis (Gale et al. 2013).

Quality Assessment

We will use the Mixed Methods Appraisal Tool (MMAT) to assess the quality of the articles (Pace et al. 2012). The appraisal will be carried out in parallel to data extraction and reviewers will input the rating into the same REDCap data extraction form. Two researchers will rate these articles independently. In cases of disagreement, the raters will discuss their responses until consensus is reached, and an additional reviewer might be added to reach a decision. Inter-rater reliability will be calculated using the kappa statistic (Landis and Koch 1977) estimated pre- and post-discussion in which $k < 0$ (poor agreement); k = 0 – 0.20 (slight agreement); k = 0.21 – 0.40 (fair agreement); k = 0.41 – 0.60 (moderate agreement); k = 0.61 – 0.80 (substantial agreement); and k = 0.81 – 1.00 (near-perfect agreement).

The findings from the review will inform data collection and analysis for the rapid ethnography.

APPENDIX D

Benefits and Limitations of Using Rapid Techniques, Divided by Rapid Technique (Vindrola-Padros and Johnson 2020)

	Elimination of Transcripts
Benefits	• Time reduction (Burgess-Allen and Owen-Smith 2010; Gravois et al. 1992; Halcombe et al. 2006; Markle et al. 2011; Neal et al. 2015; Petro 2010; Tattersall and Vernon 2007; Tessier 2012; Greenwood et al. 2017) • More robust dataset (Burgess-Allen and Owen-Smith 2010; Tessier 2012) • Increase sample size (Burgess-Allen and Owen-Smith 2010; Markle et al. 2011; Tessier 2012) • Decrease cost of research (Gravois et al. 1992; Halcombe et al. 2006; Neal et al. 2015; Tessier 2012; Greenwood et al. 2017) • Maintain nonverbal information (Gravois et al. 1992; Neal et al. 2015) • Eliminate interpretative bias of transcript production (Halcombe et al. 2006) • Increase authenticity/link with data (Markle et al. 2011; Tessier 2012) • Better match between theory and design (Halcombe et al. 2006) • Enhance transparency of data collection and analysis process (i.e. trustworthiness) (Burgess-Allen and Owen-Smith 2010; Markle et al. 2011; Neal et al. 2015)
Limitations	• May require use of additional methods (e.g. transcripts may sometimes still be needed) (Markle et al. 2011) • Reduction in natural pace of discussion/reduced interaction with facilitator (Burgess-Allen and Owen-Smith 2010; Tattersall and Vernon 2007) • Lack of depth and/or level of interpretation (Burgess-Allen and Owen-Smith 2010) • Introduction of researcher bias (Burgess-Allen and Owen-Smith 2010; Markle et al. 2011; Neal et al. 2015) • Time required to acquire new technology skills/'unlearn' a previous methodology (Markle et al. 2011; Petro 2010) • Cost of purchasing new technologies (Markle et al. 2011; Petro 2010) • Requires experienced researchers (Greenwood et al. 2017)

(cont.)

	Faster Production of Transcripts/Use of Rapid Analysis Techniques with Transcripts
Benefits	• Time reduction (Scott et al. 2009; Johnson 2011; Anderson 1998; Park and Zeanah 2005; Taylor et al. 2018; Watkins 2017)
	• Decrease cost of research (Park and Zeanah 2005)
	• Increased authenticity/link with data (Anderson 1998)
	• Enhance transparency of data collection and analysis process (i.e. trustworthiness) (Park and Zeanah 2005)
	• Limits opportunity for human error (Scott et al. 2009)
	• Physically more comfortable/better for persons with disabilities (i.e. voice recognition software) (Johnson 2011; Park and Zeanah 2005)
Limitations	• May require use of additional methods (Scott et al. 2009)
	• Requires hiring a specialty profession (Scott et al. 2009)
	• Potential loss of data (Tessier 2012)
	• Lack of sophistication of software (i.e. VAR) (Johnson 2011; Anderson 1998; Park and Zeanah 2005)
	• Voice fatigue (Anderson 1998; Park and Zeanah 2005)
	• Requires experienced researchers or researchers embedded in the research context (Taylor et al. 2018)

APPENDIX E

Draft Standards for Rapid Ethnographies and Appraisal Methods (STREAM) (originally developed by Vindrola-Padros et al., unpublished manuscript)

Section	Guideline	Description
Title and abstract	The title should be descriptive and highlight the topic under study and the type of rapid study. There should be a structured abstract with details on the aims, study design, study sample, findings, conclusions and use of findings.	
Introduction		
Rationale	Include a brief background and present the reason why the study was conducted.	It is important to specify whether the rapid study emerged out of a need recognised by the healthcare organisation or if it is commissioned by an external organisation,* as this might influence the purpose of the study and how the findings are shared.
Aim	Describe the aim of the study and purpose of the article.	
Design		
Theoretical framework and methodology	Describe the theoretical framework used to design the study and how it aligns with the methodology.	
Methods		
Research team's prior experience on the	Include information on the research team's prior	Prior experience in the organisation and/or with the

(cont.)		
Section	Guideline	Description
topic or context under study	experience on the research topic or context where the study took place.	research topic can allow researchers to reduce the amount of time required for familiarisation. The article should also specify if the research team are internal or external to the organisation where the study will take place and strategies for maintaining critical distance if the research team are also staff members from the healthcare organisation.
Study protocol	Report whether a study protocol was developed and whether there was any deviance from this during the research.	Changes in the protocol and other study materials (i.e. interview topic guides, observation guides, information sheets and consent forms) should be tracked and reported.
Data collection methods	The methods used to collect data should be presented in detail and their selection should be justified. Researchers should indicate if rapid data collection techniques were used to speed up collection and describe these in detail. If teams of field researchers are used, there should be a description of the strategies used to standardise data collection.	
Selection of research sites	Strategies for selecting research sites should be justified and the information used to inform the selection should be presented.	Representative sampling has been identified as a potential limitation in rapid research and information on sampling strategies is often missing.
Participant selection and recruitment	The process for participant selection and recruitment should be outlined.	The researchers should also specify if they used sampling frames to plan recruitment and highlight if changes in sampling needed to be made

(cont.)		
Section	Guideline	Description
		at any point due to time restrictions.
Analysis	Data analysis methods should be set out clearly and describe how the theoretical framework was used to interpret the data. Researchers should also indicate if software for data analysis was used and present the use of any rapid analytical techniques. Following guidelines for qualitative research, researchers should indicate if multiple coders were used and the strategies used to ensure consistency in the analysis (i.e. development of a team codebook, cross-checking of coding).	Rapid analytical techniques might include: for instance, instant data analysis, selected transcription or identifying themes directly from audio recordings of interviews.
Study duration	The duration of the study should be specified, including information on the amount of time spent on each phase of the research (even if these overlap as in the case of data collection and analysis). Delays produced in the study should also be reported as these represent valuable lessons for future rapid research in relation to the anticipation of potential barriers in the implementation of the study.	
Ethical considerations	Ethical principles (confidentiality, anonymity, voluntary participation, informed consent, minimise harm) should be maintained. The researchers should report approvals from ethical review boards, registration of the study with data protection offices, and informed consent processes	

(cont.)		
Section	Guideline	Description
	followed during data collection. The researchers should also indicate if ethical review processes were streamlined in any way to reduce delays in research (i.e. through expedited reviews or exemptions from full committee review).	
Findings or results		
Presentation and sharing of findings	Researchers should relate the findings to the theoretical framework. They should also include a description of the format and frequency in which findings were shared. The timing of the sharing of findings is also a determinant of the utility of rapid research and should be clearly described, including the sharing of interim findings as the research is ongoing.	
Discussion		
Interpretation and reflexivity	Interpret the findings in relation to previous research and the theoretical framework guiding the study. Researchers should reflect on their 'self-location' or positionality throughout the research and how it shaped processes of data collection and analysis. Researchers should also indicate if they used strategies proposed by qualitative research guidelines such as member checking (where participants provide feedback on the interpretation of the findings).	

(cont.)		
Section	Guideline	Description
Limitations of the study	These should be critically analysed and discussed.	It is also important for researchers to identify the reasons for these limitations (i.e. if the study was limited from the start due to short timeframes or if there were unanticipated problems encountered during fieldwork and not enough time to address them).
Summary or conclusions	Include a brief summary of the study and the main findings. The conclusions should reflect the findings of the study.	
Use/application of findings	Include a detailed description of how study findings were used (or why they could not be used).	If possible, it would also be useful to have a timeline of the application of findings, where authors indicate if findings were used to make short-term changes or changes in the long-term.

* defined as beyond the healthcare organisation where the study will take place

APPENDIX F
Outlines of Training in Rapid Research

An Introduction to Rapid Ethnography

Course Description
This practical course is intended for those interested in using rapid research methods. The course will combine short lectures with hands-on exercises. The course participants will get the opportunity to design their own rapid ethnography. A wide range of rapid research approaches will be reviewed, but the course will emphasise rapid ethnographies.

The course has the following aims:

- Introduce participants to a wide range of rapid research approaches
- Discuss the contributions and limitations of using rapid research
- Improve skills in the design and implementation of rapid appraisals and short-term ethnographies
- Improve skills in the dissemination and application of research findings

This session will cover:

- Different types of rapid ethnographies including: rapid ethnographic assessments, rapid ethnographies, short-term ethnographies, quick ethnographies and focused ethnographies
- The similarities and differences between rapid and conventional ethnographies
- The differences between lone-researcher and team-based rapid ethnographic research
- The contributions and limitations of using rapid research approaches
- The specific challenges associated with rapid ethnographies
- The steps required to design and implement rapid ethnographies
- Examples of materials that can be used to facilitate rapid data collection and analysis
- Strategies for disseminating and applying research findings

By the end of this course you will be able to:

- Differentiate between different types of rapid research approaches
- Identify instances when rapid research can be useful
- Design and implement a rapid ethnography
- Develop materials for rapid data collection and analysis
- Disseminate research findings to decision makers and other relevant stakeholders

An Introduction to Rapid Qualitative Research

This course provides an introduction to a wide range of approaches used in rapid qualitative research and rapid literature reviews. The course will combine short presentations with hands-on exercises. The participants will get the opportunity to work with real research cases and design their own rapid study. Participants who are planning a rapid study will be encouraged to use their own topic throughout the course. Short rapid research clinics will be available at the end of the course to discuss projects in detail (these will need to be pre-booked by participants).

Course Aims

1. Introduce participants to a wide range of rapid qualitative research approaches (including rapid literature reviews)
2. Discuss the contributions and limitations of using rapid qualitative research
3. Improve skills in the design and implementation of rapid qualitative research
4. Improve skills in the dissemination and application of research findings

Course Content

- Introduction to rapid research – why use rapid methods?
- Brief history of rapid research approaches
- The contributions and limitations of rapid research approaches – when are these approaches suitable?
- Overview of rapid qualitative research approaches (including rapid ethnographic assessments [REA], rapid appraisals [RA], short-term ethnographies, rapid assessment procedures [RAP])
- Step-by-step guide to designing and implementing rapid qualitative research
- The combination of rapid research with other types of research
- Rapid systematic reviews and meta-analyses
- Dissemination and the translation of findings into changes in policy and practice

Advanced Rapid Qualitative Research

This course is designed for those who have attended the introduction to rapid qualitative research course or who have experience participating in rapid qualitative studies. The aim of the course is to help attendees address issues they might be facing in the design and implementation of their rapid studies. The course combines peer work, short presentations, hands-on exercises and one-to-one coaching to review and work through the challenges encountered by researchers conducting rapid qualitative research.

Course Aims
1. Provide a brief overview of the challenges encountered by rapid qualitative researchers and strategies to address these
2. Introduce new techniques and approaches in rapid qualitative research
3. Improve skills in the design and implementation of rapid qualitative research
4. Improve skills in the dissemination and application of research findings

Course Content
- Why do we use rapid research?
- Main challenges encountered by researchers in the field
- Main challenges encountered after fieldwork has ended
- The combination of rapid research with other types of research
- New published tools in the field of rapid qualitative research
- Tools and techniques under development (the future of rapid qualitative research)

Prerequisites
- Introduction to rapid qualitative research or prior experience with rapid research

An Introduction to Rapid Evaluations

This course provides an introduction to a wide range of approaches used in the design and implementation of rapid evaluations. The course will combine short presentations with hands-on exercises. The participants will get the opportunity to work with real evaluation cases and design their own rapid evaluation. Participants who are planning a rapid study will be encouraged to use their own topic throughout the course. Short rapid research clinics will be available at the end of the course to discuss projects in detail (these will need to be pre-booked by participants).

Course Aims

1. Introduce participants to a wide range of rapid evaluation approaches
2. Discuss the contributions and limitations of using rapid evaluations
3. Improve skills in the design and implementation of rapid evaluations
4. Improve skills in the dissemination and application of evaluation findings

Course Content

- Introduction to rapid evaluations – why use rapid approaches?
- Brief history of rapid evaluations
- The contributions and limitations of rapid evaluations – when are these approaches suitable?
- Overview of rapid evaluation approaches – rapid evaluation methods (REM), rapid feedback evaluations (RFE), rapid cycle evaluations (RCE)
- Step-by-step guide to designing and implementing rapid evaluations
- The use of rapid research techniques during data collection and analysis
- Dissemination and the translation of findings into changes in policy and practice

Further Reading

Rapid Evaluation and Appraisal Methods (REAM) (Presenting General Overviews)

Anker M, Guidotti S, Orseszyna S, Thuroax M. Rapid evaluation methods (REM) of health service performance: Methodological observations. *Bulletin of the World Health Organization* 1993;71(1):15–21.

McNall M, Foster-Fishman P. Methods of rapid evaluation, assessment, and appraisal. *American Journal of Evaluation* 2007;28(2):151–168.

McNall MA, Welch VE, Ruh KL, et al. The use of rapid-feedback evaluation methods to improve the retention rates of an HIV/AIDS healthcare intervention. *Evaluation and Program Planning* 2004;27:287–294.

Nunns H. Responding to the demand for quicker evaluation findings. *Social Policy Journal of New Zealand* 2009;34:89–99.

Shrank W. The center for medicare and medicaid innovation's blueprint for rapid-cycle evaluation of new care and payment models. *Health Affairs* 2013;32:807–812.

Systematic Literature Reviews

Johnson GA, Vindrola-Padros C. Rapid qualitative research methods during complex health emergencies: A systematic review of the literature. *Social Science & Medicine* 2017;189:63–75.

Johnson GA, Vindrola-Padros C. Rapid techniques in qualitative research: A critical review of the literature. *Qualitative Health Research* 2020, doi: 10.1177/1049732320921835.

Vindrola-Padros C, Brage E, Johnson GA. Rapid, responsive and relevant? A systematic review of rapid evaluations in healthcare. *American Journal of Evaluation* 2020, doi: 10.1177/1098214019886914.

Vindrola-Padros C, Vindrola-Padros B. Quick and dirty? A systematic review of the use of rapid ethnographies in healthcare organisation and delivery. *BMJ Quality and Safety* 2018;27:321–330.

Rapid Appraisals, Rapid Qualitative Inquiry (RQI), Rapid Assessment Procedures and Process (RAP) and the RARE Model

Abramowitz S, et al. Community-centered responses to Ebola in urban Liberia: The view from below. *PLoS Neglected Tropical Diseases* 2015;9(4):e0003706.

Beebe J. Basic concepts and techniques of rapid appraisal. *Human Organization* 1995;54 (1):42–51.

Beebe, J. *Rapid Assessment Process: An Introduction.* Oxford: AltaMira Press; 2001.

Beebe J. *Rapid Qualitative Inquiry.* Second edn. London: Rowman and Littlefield; 2014.

Beebe J. Rapid assessment process. In: Kempf-Leonard K, editor. *Encyclopedia of Social Measurement.* New York: Elsevier; 2005: 285–291.

Brown, D., et al. A participatory action research pilot study of urban health disparities using rapid assessment response and evaluation. *American Journal of Public Health* 2008;98(1):28–38. THIS IS THE ARTICLE THAT HAS EXAMPLES OF THE RAP SHEET

Chambers R. Participatory rural appraisal: Analysis of experience. *World Development* 1994a;22(9):1253–1268.

Chambers R. The origins and practice of participatory rural appraisal. *World Development* 1994b;22(7):953–969. THIS IS THE ARTICLE THAT LISTS THE 29 METHODS.

Fitch C, Rhodes T, Stimson G. Origins of an epidemic: The methodological and political emergence of rapid assessment. *International Journal of Drug Policy* 2000;11:63–82.

Harris K, Jerome N, Fawcett S. Rapid assessment procedures: A review and critique. *Human Organization* 1997;56(3):375–378.

Manderson L, Aaby P. Can rapid anthropological procedures be applied to tropical diseases? *Health Policy and Planning* 1992a;7(1):46–55.

Manderson L, Aaby P. An epidemic in the field? Rapid assessment procedures and health research. *Social Science & Medicine* 1992b;35(7):839–850.

McMullen C., et al. Rapid assessment of clinical information systems in the healthcare setting: An efficient method for time-pressed evaluation. *Methods of Information in Medicine* 2011;50(4):299–307.

Rifkin S. Rapid appraisals for health: An overview. *Rapid Rural Appraisal Notes* 1992;16:7–12.

Scrimshaw S, Hurtado E. Anthropological involvement on the Central American diarrheal disease control project. *Social Science & Medicine* 1988;27(1):97–105.

Trotter RTII, Needle RH, Goosby E, Bates C, Singer M. A methodological model for rapid assessment, response, and evaluation: The RARE program in public health. *Field Methods* 2001:13(2):137–159.

Utarini A, Winkvist A, Pelto G. Appraising studies in health using rapid assessment procedures (RAP): Eleven critical criteria. *Human Organization* 2001;60(4):390–400.

Rapid Ethnographies (General Descriptions of the Approach)

Bentley M, Pelto G, Straus W, Schumann D, Adegbola C, de la Pena E, et al. Rapid ethnographic assessment: Applications in diarrhea management program. *Social Science & Medicine* 1988;27(1):107–116.

Cruz E, Higginbottom G. The use of focused ethnography in nursing research. *Nurse Researcher* 2013;20(4):36–43.

Handwerker P. *Quick Ethnography: A Guide to Rapid Multi-Method Research*. Lanham, MD: AltaMira Press; 2001.

Knoblauch H. Focused ethnography. *Forum: Qualitative Social Research* 2005;6(3):1–13.

Pink S, Morgan J. Short-term ethnography: Intense routes to knowing. *Symbolic Interaction* 2013;36(3):351–361.

Rapid Tools to Speed Up Data Collection or Analysis

Anderson J. Transcribing with voice recognition software: A new tool for qualitative researchers. *Qualitative Health Research* 1998;8(5):718–723.

Burgess-Allen J, Owen-Smith V. Using mind mapping techniques for rapid qualitative data analysis in public participation processes. *Health Expect* 2010;13:406–415.

Gravois T, Rosenfield S, Greenberg B. Establishing reliability for coding implementation concerns of school-based teams from audiotapes. *Evaluation Review* 1992;16 (5):562–569.

Greenwood M, Kendrick T, Davies H, Gill F. Hearing voices: Comparing two methods for analysis of focus group data. *Applied Nursing Research* 2017;35:90–93.

Halcomb EJ, Davidson PM. Is verbatim transcription of interview data always necessary? *Applied Nursing Research* 2006;19(1):38–42.

Joe J, Chaudhuri S, Le T, Thompson H, Demiris G. The use of think-aloud and instant data analysis in evaluation research: Exemplar and lessons learned. *Journal of Biomedical Informatics* 2015;56:284–291.

Johnson B. The speed and accuracy of voice recognition software-assisted transcription versus the listen-and-type method: A research note. *Qualitative Research* 2011;11 (1):91–97.

Lopez KD, Febretti A, Stifter J, Johnson A, Wilkie DJ, Keenan G. Toward a more robust and efficient usability testing method of clinical decision support for nurses derived from nursing electronic health record data. *International Journal of Nursing Knowledge* 2017;28(4):211–218.

Markle T, West R, Rich P. Beyond transcription: Technology, change and refinement of method. *Forum: Qualitative Social Research* 2011;12(3):art. 21.

Neal J, Neal Z, VanDyke E, Kornbluh M. Expediting the analysis of qualitative data in evaluation: A procedure for the rapid identification of themes from audio recordings (RITA). *American Journal of Evaluation* 2015;36(1):118–132.

Park J, Zeanah E. An evaluation of voice recognition software for use in interview-based research: A research note. *Qualitative Research* 2005;5(2):245–251.

Petro N. Hate taking notes? Try mind mapping. *GP Solo* 2010:21–23.

Scott SD, Sharpe H, O'Leary K, Dehaeck U, Hindmarsh K, Moore JG, Osmond MH. Court reporters: A viable solution for the challenges of focus group data collection? *Qualitative Health Research* 2009;19(1):140–146.

Tattersall C, Vernon S. Mind mapping as a tool in qualitative research. *Nursing Times* 2007;103(26):32–33.

Taylor B, Henshall C, Kenyon S, Litchfield I, Greenfield S. Can rapid approaches to qualitative analysis deliver timely, valid findings to clinical leaders? A mixed methods study comparing rapid and thematic analysis. *BMJ Open* 2018:e019993.

Tessier S. From field notes to transcripts to tape recordings: Evolution or combination? *International Journal of Qualitative Methods* 2012;11(4):446–460.

Watkins D. Rapid and rigorous qualitative data analysis: The 'RADaR' technique for applied research. *International Journal of Qualitative Methods* 2017;16:1–9.

Rapid Evaluations

Anker M, Guidotti RJ, Orzeszyna S, Sapirie S. A, Thuriaux MC. Rapid evaluation methods (REM) of health services performance: Methodological observations. *Bulletin of the World Health Organization* 1993;71(1):15–21.

Aspray TJ, Nesbit K, Cassidy TP, Hawthorne G. Rapid assessment methods used for health-equity audit: Diabetes mellitus among frail British care-home residents. *Public Health* 2006;120(11):1042–1051.

Bjornson-Benson WM, Stibolt TB, Manske KA, Zavela KJ, Youtsey DJ, Buist AS. Monitoring recruitment effectiveness and cost in a clinical trial. *Controlled Clinical Trials* 1993;14(2 Suppl):52S–67S.

Chowdhury SNM, Moni D. A situation analysis of the menstrual regulation programme in Bangladesh. *Reproductive Health Matters* 2004;12(24 Suppl):95–104.

Felisberto E, Freese E, Natal S, Alves CK de A. [A contribution to institutionalized health evaluation: A proposal for self-evaluation]. *Cadernos de saude publica* 2008;24 (9):2091–2102.

Gale R, Wu J, Erhardt, T, Bounthavong M, Reardon C, Damschroder L, Midboe A. Comparison of rapid vs in-depth qualitative analytic methods from a process evaluation of academic detailing in the Veterans Health Administration. *Implementation Science* 2019;14:11.

Glasgow, R. et al. Conducting rapid, relevant research lessons learned from the my own health report project. *American Journal of Preventive Medicine* 2014;47(2):212–219.

Grant, L., et al. Palliative care making a difference in rural Uganda, Kenya and Malawi: Three rapid evaluation field studies. *BMC Palliative Care* 2011;10:8.

Grasso, P. What makes an evaluation useful? Reflections from experience in large organizations. *American Journal of Evaluation* 2003;24(4):507–514.

Keith, R. Using the Consolidated Framework for Implementation Research (CFIR) to produce actionable findings: A rapid-cycle evaluation approach to improving implementation. *Implementation Science* 2017;12:15.

McNall M, Welch V, Ruh K, Mildner C, Soto T. The use of rapid-feedback evaluation methods to improve the retention rates of an HIV/AIDS healthcare intervention. *Evaluation and Program Planning* 2004;27:287–294.

Munday, D. et al. Rural palliative care in North India: Rapid evaluation of a program using a realist mixed method approach. *Indian Journal of Palliative Care* 2018;24(1):3–8.

Nunns, H. Responding to the demand for quicker evaluation findings. *Social Policy Journal of New Zealand* 2009;34:89–99.

Riley, W., et al. Rapid, responsive, relevant (R3) research: A call for a rapid learning health research enterprise. *Clinical and Translational Science* 2013;2:10.

Sandison, P. Desk-based review of real-time evaluation experience. *UNICEF* 2003.

Schneeweiss S, Shrank WH, Ruhl M, Maclure M. Decision-making aligned with rapid-cycle evaluation in health care. *International Journal of Technology Assessment in Health Care* 2015;31:214–222.

Shrank W. The Center for Medicare and Medicaid Innovation's blueprint for rapid-cycle evaluation of new care and payment models. *Health Affairs* 2013;32(4):807–812.

Skillman, M. et al. A framework for rigorous qualitative research as a component of mixed method rapid-cycle evaluation. *Qualitative Health Research* 2019;29 (2):279–289.

Taylor B, Henshall C, Kenyon S, et al. Can rapid approaches to qualitative analysis deliver timely, valid findings to clinical leaders? A mixed methods study comparing rapid and thematic analysis. *BMJ Open* 2018;8:e019993.

Zakocs R, Hill JA, Brown P, Wheaton J, Freire KE. The data-to-action framework: A rapid program improvement process. *Health Education & Behavior: The Official Publication of the Society for Public Health Education* 2015;42(4):471–479.

Rapid Systematic Reviews or Evidence Syntheses

Tricco A, et al. A scoping review of rapid review methods. *BMC Medicine* 2015;13:224.

Tricco A, et al. *Rapid Reviews to Strengthen Health Policy and Systems: A Practical Guide.* Geneva: World Health Organization; 2017.

References

Abramowitz S, McLean K, McKune S, Bardosh S, Fallah M, Monger J, Tehoungue K, Omidian P. Community-centered responses to Ebola in urban Liberia: The view from below. *PLoS Neglected Tropical Diseases* 2015;9(4):e0003706.

Abramson CM, Dohan D. Beyond text: Using arrays to represent and analyze ethnographic data. *Sociological Methodology* 2015;45(1):272–319.

Abu-Lughod L. Writing against culture. In: *Recapturing Anthropology: Working in the Present*, Fox RG, editor. Santa Fe, NM: School of American Research Press; 1991:137–162.

Afonja S. Rapid assessment methodologies: Application to health and nutrition programmes in Africa. In: *Rapid Assessment Methodologies: Qualitative Methodologies for Planning and Evaluation of Health Related Programs*, Scrimshaw N, Gleason G, editors. Boston: International Nutrition Foundation for Developing Countries (INFDC); 1992:81–94.

Agyepong IA, Aryee B, Dzikunu H, Manderson L. *The Malaria Manual: Guidelines for the Rapid Assessment of Social, Economic and Cultural Aspects of Malaria*. Geneva: United Nations Development Programme, World Bank, World Health Organization Special Program for Research and Training in Tropical Disease (TDR); 1995.

Agyepong IA, Manderson L. The diagnosis and management of fever at household level in the Greater Accra Region, Ghana. *Acta Tropica* 1994;58(3–4):317–330.

Amit V. Introduction: Constructing the field. In: *Constructing the Field: Ethnographic Fieldwork in the Contemporary World*, V. Amit, editor. London: Routledge; 2000:1–18.

Anderson J. Transcribing with voice recognition software: A new tool for qualitative researchers. *Qualitative Health Research* 1998;8(5):718–723.

Anker M, Guidotti S, Orseszyna S, Thuroax M. Rapid evaluation methods (REM) of health service performance: Methodological observations. *Bulletin of the World Health Organization* 1993;71(1):15–21.

Anspach R, Mizrachi N. The field worker's fields: Ethics, ethnography and medical sociology. *Sociology of Health and Illness* 2006;28(6):713–731.

Appadurai A. Putting hierarchy in its place. *Cultural Anthropology* 1988;3:36–49.

Aral S, St. Lawrence J, Dyatlov R. Commercial sex work, drug use, and sexually transmitted infections in St. Petersburg, Russia. *Social Science & Medicine* 2005;60:2181–2190.

Armstrong P, Armstrong H. Theory matters. In: *Creative Teamwork: Developing Rapid, Site-Switching Ethnography*, Armstrong P, Lowndes R, editor. Oxford: Oxford University Press; 2018:1–20.

Armstrong P, Lowndes R. *Creative Teamwork: Developing Rapid, Site-Switching Ethnography*. Oxford: Oxford University Press; 2018.

Ash JS, Sittig DF, Dykstra R, Wright A, McMullen C, Richardson J, et al. Identifying best practices for clinical decision support and knowledge management in the field. *Studies in Health Technology and Informatics* 2010;160(Pt 2):806–810.

Ash JS, Sittig DF, Guappone KP, Dykstra RH, Richardson J, Wright A, et al. Recommended practices for computerized clinical decision support and knowledge management in community settings: A qualitative study. *BMC Medical Informatics and Decision Making* 2012;12:1–19.

Baim-Lance A, Vindrola-Padros C. Reconceptualising 'impact' through anthropology's ethnographic practices. *Anthropology in Action* 2015;22 (2):5–13.

Baines D, Gnanayutham R. Rapid ethnography and a knowledge mobilization project: Benefits from bookettes. In: *Creative Teamwork: Developing Rapid, Site-Switching Ethnography*, Armstrong P, Lowndes R, editor. Oxford: Oxford University Press; 2018:156–170.

Bate SP. Whatever happened to organizational anthropology? *Human Relations* 1997;50:1147–1171.

Bauman AE, Nelson DE, Pratt M, Matsudo V, Schoeppe S. Dissemination of physical activity evidence, programs, policies, and surveillance in the international public health arena. *American Journal of Preventive Medicine* 2006;31(1 Suppl):S57–S65.

Beebe J. Basic concepts and techniques of rapid appraisal. *Human Organization* 1995;54(1):42–51.

Beebe J. *Rapid Assessment Process: An Introduction.* Walnut Creek, CA: AltaMira Press; 2001.

Beebe J. Rapid assessment process. In: *Encyclopedia of Social Measurement.* Kempf-Leonard K, editor. New York: Elsevier Limited; 2004:285–291.

Beebe J. *Rapid Qualitative Inquiry.* Second edn. London: Rowman and Littlefield; 2014.

Bentley M, Pelto G, Straus W, Schumann D, Adegbola C, de la Pena E, et al. Rapid ethnographic assessment: Applications in diarrhea management program. *Social Science & Medicine* 1988;27(1):107–116.

Bernard HR. *Research Methods in Anthropology: Qualitative and Quantitative Approaches*, 4th edn. Oxford: AltaMira Press; 2006.

Bikker A, Atherton H, Brant H, Porqueddu T, Campbell J, Gibson A, McKinstry B, Salisbury C, Ziebland S. Conducting a team-based multi-sited focused ethnography in primary care. *BMC Medical Research Methodology* 2017;17:139.

Bjornson-Benson WM, Stibolt TB, Manske KA, Zavela KJ, Youtsey DJ, Buist AS. Monitoring recruitment effectiveness and cost in a clinical trial. *Controlled Clinical Trials* 1993;14(2 Suppl):52S–67S.

Bond G. Fieldnotes: Research in past occurrences. In: *Fieldnotes: The Makings of Anthropology*, Sanjek R, editor. Ithaca: Cornell University Press; 1990:273–289.

Bowen S, Bottling I, Graham I, et al. Experience of health leadership in partnering with university-based researchers in Canada-A call to 're-imagine' research. *International Journal of Health Policy Management* 2019;8(12):684–699.

Boyd J, Collins A, Mayer S, Maher L, Kerr T, McNeil R. Gendered violence and overdose prevention sites: A rapid ethnographic study during an overdose epidemic in Vancouver, Canada. *Addiction* 2018;113:2261–2270.

Braedley S. Ethics as teamwork. In: *Creative Teamwork: Developing Rapid, Site-Switching Ethnography*, Armstrong P, Lowndes R, editors. Oxford: Oxford University Press; 2018:37–52.

Brown D, Hernandez A, Saint-Jean G, Evans S, Tafari I, Brewster L, Celestin M, Gomez-Estefan C, Regalado F, Akal S, Nierenberg B, Kauschinger E, Schwartz R, Page B. A participatory action research pilot study of urban health disparities using rapid assessment response and evaluation. *American Journal of Public Health* 2008;98(1):28–38.

Bryman A. *Social Research Methods*, 2nd edn. Oxford: Oxford University Press; 2004.

Burgess-Allen J, Owen-Smith V. Using mind mapping techniques for rapid qualitative data analysis in public participation processes. *Health Expectations* 2010;13:406–415.

Canadian Health Services Research Foundation (CHSRF). *Communication Notes. Developing a Dissemination Plan.* Ottawa: Canadian Health Services Research Foundation; 2004.

Chambers, R. Shortcut methods in information gathering for rural development projects. In: Proceedings of the Agricultural Sector Symposia, 7–11 January 1980, pp. 393–410. World Bank.

Chambers R. Rapid rural appraisal: Rationale and repertoire. *Public Administration Development* 1981;1:95–106.

Chambers R. *Rural Appraisal: Rapid, Relaxed and Participatory*. London: Institute of Development Studies; 1992.

Chambers R. The origins and practice of participatory rural appraisal. *World Development* 1994;22(7):953–969.

Chambers R. PRA, PLA and pluralism: Practice and theory. In: *The SAGE Handbook of Action Research: Participative Inquiry and Practice*, Reason P, Bradbury H, editor. Thousand Oaks, CA: SAGE; 2008:297–318.

Chambers R, Blackburn J. *The Power of Participation. IDS Policy Briefing Issue.* Brighton, England: Institute of Development Students, University of Sussex; 1996.

Clifford J. On ethnographic authority. *Representations* 1983;2:118–146.

Coffey, A. The power of accounts: Authority and authorship in ethnography. *International Journal of Qualitative Studies in Education* 1996;9(1):61–74.

Coleman S, Collins P. Introduction: 'Being . . . where?' Performing fields on shifting grounds. In: *Locating the Field: Space, Place and Context in Anthropology*, Coleman S, Collins P, editors. Oxford: Berg; 2006:1–21.

Coleman S, von Hellerman P, editors. *Multi-sited Ethnography: Problems and Possibilities in the Translocation of Research Methods*. London: Routledge; 2009.

Coreil J, Augustin A, Holt E, Halsey NA. Use of ethnographic research for instrument development in a case-control study of immunization use in Haiti. *International Journal of Epidemiology* 1989;18(4 Suppl 2):S33–S37.

Creese A, Bhatt A, Bhojan N, Martin P. Fieldnotes in team ethnography: Researching complementary schools. *Qualitative Research* 2008;8(2): 197–215.

Cruz EV, Higginbottom G. The use of focused ethnography in nursing research. *Nurse Researcher* 2013;20(4):36–43.

Culhane-Pera KA, Sriphetcharawut S, Thawsirichuchai R, Yangyuenkun W, Kunstadter P. Afraid of delivering at the hospital or afraid of delivering at home: A qualitative study of Thai Hmong families' decision-making about maternity services. *Maternal and Child Health Journal* 2015;19(11):2384–2392.

Cupit C, Mackintosh N, Armstrong N. Using ethnography to study improving healthcare: Reflections on the 'ethnographic' label. *BMJ Quality & Safety* 2018 Feb 20; Available from: http://qualitysafety.bmj.com/content/early/2018/02/20/bmjqs-2017-007599 .abstract

Dalakoglou D, Harvey P. Roads and anthropology: Ethnographic perspectives on space, time and (im)mobility. *Mobilities* 2012;7(4):459–465.

de Meyrick J. The Delphi method and health research. *Health Education Journal* 2003;103:7–16.

Desmond N, Allen C, Clift S, Justine B, Mzugu J, Plummer M, et al. A typology of groups at risk of HIV/STI in a gold mining town in north-western Tanzania. *Social Science & Medicine* 2005;60:1739–1749.

Driscoll A, Currey J, Worrall-Carter L, Stewart S. Ethical dilemmas of a large national multi-centre study in Australia: Time for some consistency. *Journal of Clinical Nursing* 2008;17(16):2212–2220.

Dupuis-Blanchard S, Neufeld A, Strang VT. The significance of social engagement in relocated older adults. *Qualitative Health Research* 2009;19(9):1186–1195.

Eaton K, Stritzke W, Ohan J. Using scribes in qualitative research as an alternative to transcription. *The Qualitative Report* 2019;24(3):586–605.

Economic and Social Research Council (ESRC). *Communications Strategy: A Step-by-Step Guide.* Swindon: Economic and Social Research Council; 2004.

Eden G, Sharma S, Roy D, Joshi A, Nocera J, Tangaswamy N. Field trip as method: A rapid fieldwork approach. Proceedings of India HCI Conference, 1–3 November 2019. https://doi.org/10.1145/3364183.3364188.

Ensign J, Bell M. Illness experiences of homeless youth. *Qualitative Health Research* 2004;14(9):1239–1254.

Etchells E, Ho M, Shojania KG. Value of small sample sizes in rapid-cycle quality improvement projects. *BMJ Quality & Safety* 2016;25:202–206.

Faubion, J. The ethics of fieldwork as an ethics of connectivity, or the good anthropologist (isn't what she used to be). In: *Fieldwork Is Not What It Used to Be: Learning Anthropology's Method in a Time of Transition*, Faubion J and Marcus G, editors. Ithaca: Cornell University Press; 2009:145–166.

Fitch C, Rhodes T, Stimson G. Origins of an epidemic: The methodological and political emergence of rapid assessment. *International Journal of Drug Policy* 2000;11:63–82.

Fluehr-Lobban C. *Ethics and the Profession of Anthropology: Dialogue for a New Era.* Philadelphia: University of Pennsylvania Press; 1991.

Fudge N, Redfern J, Wolfe C, McKevitt C. Streamlined Research Governance: Are We There Yet? *BMJ* 2010;341:635–637.

Fulop N, Capelas Barbosa E, Hill M, Ledger J, Sherlaw-Johnson C, Spencer J, et al. Special measures for quality and challenged providers: Study protocol for evaluating the impact of improvement interventions in NHS trusts. *International Journal of Health Policy and Management* 2019, doi:10.15171/ijhpm.2019.100

Gale NK, Heath G, Cameron E, Rashid S, Redwood S. Using the framework method for the analysis of qualitative data in multidisciplinary health research. *BMC Medical Research Methodology* 2013;13:117.

Gale, R., et al. Comparison of rapid vs in-depth qualitative analytic methods from a process evaluation of academic detailing in the Veterans Health Administration. *Implementation Science* 2019;14:11.

Garcia CM, Saewyc EM. Perceptions of mental health among recently immigrated Mexican adolescents. *Issues in Mental Health Nursing* 2007;28(1):37–54.

Garko SB. Sexual and family planning practices and needs of people living with HIV/AIDS in Nigeria: A rapid ethnographic assessment. *Annals of African Medicine* 2007;6:124–127.

Garrett J, Downen J. Strengthening rapid assessments in urban areas: Lessons from Bangladesh and Tanzania. *Human Organization* 2002;61(4):314–327.

Geertz C. *Works and Lives: The Anthropologist as Author.* Stanford: Stanford University Press; 1988.

Gittelsohn J, Pelto P, Bentley M, Bhattacharyya K, Jensen J. *Rapid Assessment Procedures (RAP): Ethnographic Methods to Investigate Women's Health.* Boston: International Nutrition Foundation; 1998.

Goepp JG, Chin NP, Malia T, Poordabbagh A. Planning emergency medical services for children in Bolivia: Part 2 – results of a rapid assessment procedure. *Pediatric Emergency Care* 2004;20(10):664–670.

Goepp JG, Meykler S, Mooney NE, Lyon C, Raso R, Julliard K. Provider insights about palliative care barriers and facilitators: Results of a rapid ethnographic assessment. *American Journal of Hospital Palliative Care* 2008;25(4):309–314.

Goodman D, Ogrinc G, Davies L, et al. Explanation and elaboration of the SQUIRE (Standards for Quality Improvement Reporting Excellence) guidelines, v. 2.0: Examples of SQUIRE elements in the healthcare improvement literature. *BMJ Quality & Safety* 2016;25:7.

Gravois T, Rosenfield S, Greenberg B. Establishing reliability for coding implementation concerns of school-based teams from audiotapes. *Evaluation Review* 1992;16(5):562–569.

Green L, Lowery J, Kowalski C, Wyszewianski L. Impact of Institutional Review Board practice variation on observational health services research. *Health Services Research* 2006;41(1):215–230.

Greenwood M, Kendrick T, Davies H, Gill F. Hearing voices: Comparing two methods for analysis of focus group data. *Applied Nursing Research* 2017;35:90–93.

Gubrium J, Holstein J. *Analyzing Narrative Reality.* Los Angeles: SAGE; 2009.

Guerrero M, Morrow R, Calva J, Ortega-Gallegos H, Weller S, Ruiz-Palacios G, et al. Rapid ethnographic assessment of breastfeeding practices in periurban Mexico City. *Bulletin of the World Health Organization* 1999;77(4):323–330.

Gupta A, Ferguson J. *Anthropological Locations: Boundaries and Grounds of a Field Science*. Berkeley: University of California Press; 1997.

Halcomb EJ, Davidson PM. Is verbatim transcription of interview data always necessary? *Applied Nursing Research* 2006;19(1):38–42.

Halme M, Kourula A, Lindeman S, Kallio G, Lima-Toivanen M. Sustainability innovation at the base of the pyramid through multi-sited rapid ethnography. *Corporate Social Responsibility and Environmental Management* 2016;23:113–128.

Handwerker P. *Quick Ethnography: A Guide to Rapid Multi-Method Research*. Lanham: Rowman AltaMira; 2001.

Hargreaves MB. Rapid evaluation methods from complex initiatives. HHS Office of the Secretary for Planning and Evaluation issue brief. Available from: http://aspe.hhs .gov/sp/reports/2014/EvalApproach/rs_EvalApproach.cfm.

Harris K, Jerome N, Fawcett S. Rapid assessment procedures: A review and critique. *Human Organization* 1997;56(3):375–378.

Harte JD, Sheehan A, Stewart SC, Foureur M. Childbirth supporters' experiences in a built hospital birth environment. *Health Environments Research & Design Journal* 2016;9 (3):135–161.

Hasson F, Keeney S, McKenna H. Research guidelines for the Delphi survey technique. *Journal of Advanced Nursing* 2000;32:1008–1015.

Hegel C, Cantarella L, Marcus G. *Ethnography by Design: Scenographic Experiments in Fieldwork*. New York: Bloomsbury Publishing; 2019.

Herman E, Bentley M. *Rapid Assessment Procedures (RAP) to Improve the Household Management of Diarrhea*. Boston: International Foundation for Developing Countries; 1993.

Heywood P. W(h)ither Rapid (Rural) Appraisal techniques in nutrition. Unpublished manuscript, Brisbane; 1990.

Higginbottom GMA. The transitioning experiences of internationally-educated nurses into a Canadian health care system: A focused ethnography. *BMC Nursing* 2011;10 (14):1–13.

Hildebrand P. Summary of the sondeo methodology used by ICTA. Paper presented at the Rapid Rural Appraisal Conference at the Institute of Development Studies, University of Sussex, Brighton, England; 1979.

Hine C. *Ethnography for the Internet: Embedded, Embodied and Everyday*. New York: Bloomsbury Publishing; 2015.

Hundt GL, Stuttaford M, Ngoma B, SASPI Team. The social diagnostics of stroke-like symptoms: Healers, doctors and prophets in Agincourt, Limpopo Province, South Africa. *Journal of Biosocial Science* 2004;36(4):433–443.

Iedema R, Allen S, Britton K, Hor S. Out of the frying pan? Streamlining the ethics review process of multisite qualitative research projects. *Australian Health Review* 2012;37 (2):137–139.

Jackson J. I am a fieldnote: Fieldnotes as a symbol of professional identity. In: *Fieldnotes: The Makings of Anthropology*, Sanjek R, editor. Ithaca: Cornell University Press; 1990:3–33.

Jackson J. Changes in fieldnotes practice over the past thirty years in U.S. anthropology. In *eFieldnotes: The Makings of Anthropology in the Digital World*, Sanjek R, Tratner S, editors. Philadelphia: University of Pennsylvania Press; 2016:42–64.

Jamal A, Crisp J. *Real-Time Humanitarian Evaluation: Some Frequently Asked Questions.* Geneva: UNHCR; 2002.

Jarzabkowski P, Bednarek, R, Cabantous L. Conducting global team-based ethnography: Methodological challenges and practical methods. *Human Relations* 2015;68(1):3–33.

Jeffrey B, Troman G. Time for ethnography. *British Educational Research Journal* 2004;30(4):535–548.

Johnson B. The speed and accuracy of voice recognition software-assisted transcription versus the listen-and-type method: A research note. *Qualitative Research* 2011;11(1):91–97.

Johnson, GA, Vindrola-Padros C, Cooper S, Djellouli N. Tools and practical approaches: Rapid anthropological assessments in the field. OFDA; 2019. Available from: www .socialscienceinaction.org/

Johnson GA, Vindrola-Padros C. Rapid qualitative research methods during complex health emergencies: A systematic review of the literature. *Social Science & Medicine* 2017;189:63–75.

Jowsey T. Watering down ethnography. *BMJ Quality & Safety* 2016;25(7):554–555.

Khan S. The subpoena of ethnographic data. *Sociological Forum* 2019;34(1):253–263.

Kilian C, Salmoni A, Ward-Griffin C et al. Perceiving falls within a family context: A focused ethnographic approach. *Canadian Journal on Aging* 2008;27 (4): 331–345.

Kilo C. A framework for collaborative improvement: Lessons from the institute for Healthcare Improvement's Breakthrough Series. *Quality Management in Health Care* 1998;6(4):1–13.

Kirsch H. The use of rapid assessment procedures: Focus groups and small-scale surveys for community programs. In: *Drug Lessons and Education Programs in Developing Countries*, Kirsch H, editor. New Brunswick: Transaction Publishers; 1995:91–104.

Kluwin T, Morris C, Clifford J. A rapid ethnography of itinerant teachers of the deaf. *American Annals of the Deaf* 2004;149(1):62–72.

Knoblauch, H. Focused ethnography. *Forum Qualitative Sozialforschung / Forum: Qualitative Social Research* 2005;6(3):Art. 44, http://nbn-resolving.de/urn:nbn: de:0114-fqs0503440 (accessed 1 May 2014).

Knoblauch R, Tuma R, Schnettler B. *Videography: Introduction to Interpretive Videoanalysis of Social Situations.* New York: Peter Lang; 2014.

Kontos PC, Naglie G. Expressions of personhood in Alzheimer's: Moving from ethnographic text to performing ethnography. *Qualitative Research* 2006; 6(3):301–317.

Kozinets RV. *Netography: Doing Ethnographic Research Online.* London: SAGE; 2010.

Kresno S, Harrison G, Sutrisna B, Reingold A. Acute respiratory illnesses in children under five years in Indramayu, West Java, Indonesia: A rapid ethnographic assessment. *Medical Anthropology* 1993;15:4:425–434.

Landis JR, Koch GG. The measurement of observer agreement for categorical data. *Biometrics* 1977;33(1):159–174.

Lassiter LE. Collaborative ethnography and public anthropology. *Current Anthropology* 2005;46(1):83–106.

Lassiter LE. Moving past public anthropology and doing collaborative research. *NAPA Bulletin* 2008;29:70–86.

LeCompte M, Schensul J. *Ethics in Ethnography: A Mixed-Methods Approach*. Lanham: AltaMira Press; 2015.

Lewis S, Hudson M, Painter J. Revealing a 'hidden civil war': A serendipitous methodology. In: *Messy Ethnographies in Action: Tales from the Field*, Plows A, editor. Wilmington: Vernon Press; 2018:13–22.

Lewis S, Russell A. Being embedded: A way forward for ethnographic research. *Ethnography* 2011;12(3):398–416.

Long A, Scrimshaw SCM, Hurtado E. *Epilepsy Rapid Assessment Procedures (ERAP): Rapid Assessment Procedures for the Evaluation of Epilepsy Specific Beliefs, Attitudes and Behaviours*. Landover: Epilepsy Foundation of America; 1988.

Lopez KD, Febretti A, Stifter J, Johnson A, Wilkie DJ, Keenan G. Toward a more robust and efficient usability testing method of clinical decision support for nurses derived from nursing electronic health record data. *International Journal of Nursing Knowledge* 2017;28(4):211–218.

Lowndes R, Storm P, Szebehely M. Fieldnotes: Individual versus team-based rapid ethnography. In: *Creative Teamwork: Developing Rapid, Site-Switching Ethnography*, Armstrong P, Lowndes R, editors. Oxford: Oxford University Press; 2018:81–95.

Luduena AC, Olson JK, Pasco, AC. Promoción de la salud y calidad de vida entre madres de preadolescentes: Una etnografia enfocada. *Revista Latino-Americana Enfermagem* [online]. 2005;13(2):1127–1134.

Madison S. *Performed Ethnography and Communication: Improvisation and Embodied Experience*. Oxford: Routledge; 2018.

Mallick A, O'Callaghan F. Research governance delays for a multicentre non-interventional study. *Journal of the Royal Society of Medicine* 2009;102:195–198.

Manderson L, Aaby P. An epidemic in the field? Rapid assessment procedures and health research. *Social Science & Medicine* 1992a;35(7):839–850.

Manderson L, Aaby P. Can rapid anthropological procedures be applied to tropical diseases? *Health Policy and Planning* 1992b;7(1):46–55.

Mannay D, Morgan M. Doing ethnography or applying a qualitative technique? Reflections from the 'waiting field'. *Qualitative Research* 2015;15(2):166–182.

Marcus G. Ethnography in/of the world system: The emergence of multi-sited ethnography. *Annual Review of Anthropology* 1995;24(1):95–117.

Marcus, G. Multi-sited ethnography: Five or six things I know about it now. In: *Multi-Sited Ethnography: Problems and Possibilities in the Translocation of Research Methods*, Coleman S, von Hellermann P, editors. New York: Routledge; 2006:16–34.

Marcus G. Notes toward an ethnographic memoir of supervising graduate research through anthropology's decades of transformation. In: *Fieldwork Is Not What It Used to Be: Learning Anthropology's Method in a Time of Transition*, Faubion J, Marcus G, editors. Ithaca: Cornell University Press; 2009:1–36.

Markle T, West R, Rich P. Beyond transcription: Technology, change and refinement of method. *Forum: Qualitative Social Research* 2011;12(3):art. 21.

Mauthner NS, Doucet A. Knowledge once divided can be hard to put together again: An epistemological critique of collaborative and team-based research practices. *Sociology* 2008;42(5):971–985.

Mayer S, Boyd J, Collins A, Kennedy M, Fairbairn N, McNeil R. Characterizing fentanyl-related overdoses and implications for overdose response: Findings from a rapid ethnographic study in Vancouver, Canada. *Drug and Alcohol Dependence* 2018;193:69–74.

McDonach E, Barbour R, Williams B. Reflections on applying for NHS ethical approval and governance in a climate of rapid change: Prioritizing process over principles. *International Journal of Social Research Methodology* 2009;12(3):227–241.

McKeown M, Thomson G, Scholes A, Jones F, Downe S, Price O, Baker J, Greenwood P, Whittington R, Duxbury J. Restraint minimisation in mental health care: Legitimate or illegitimate force? An ethnographic study. *Sociology of Health and Illness* 2020, doi:10.1111/1467-9566.13015.

McNall M, Foster-Fishman P. Methods of rapid evaluation, assessment, and appraisal. *American Journal of Evaluation* 2007;28(2):151–168.

McNall M, Welch V, Ruh K, Mildner C, Soto T. The use of rapid-feedback evaluation methods to improve the retention rates of an HIV/AIDS healthcare intervention. *Evaluation and Program Planning* 2004;27:287–294.

Mezinska S, Kakuk P, Mijaljica G, et al. Research in disaster settings: A systematic qualitative review of ethical guidelines. *BMC Medical Ethics* 2016;17:62.

Millum J, Menikoff J. Streamlining ethical review. *Annals of Internal Medicine* 2010;153 (10):655–657.

Moher D, Liberati A, Tetzlaff J, Altman DG. Preferred reporting items for systematic reviews and meta-analyses: The PRISMA statement. *BMJ* 2009;339:b2535.

Moher D, Schulz K, Simera I, Altman D. Guidance for developers of health research reporting guidelines. *PLoS Medicine* 2010;7(2):1000217.

Muecke MA. On the evaluation of ethnographies. In: *Critical Issues in Qualitative Research Methods*, Morse JM, editor. Thousand Oaks: Sage Publications; 1994:187–209.

Mullaney T, Pettersson H, Nyholm T, Stolterman E. Thinking beyond the cure: A case for human-centered design in cancer care. *International Journal of Design* 2012;6(3):n/a.

Munoz-Plaza CE, Parry C, Hahn EE, Tang T, Nguen HQ, Gould MK, Kanter MH, Sharp AL. Integrating qualitative research methods into care improvement efforts within a learning health system: Addressing antibiotic overuse. *Health Research Policy and Systems* 2016;14:63.

Murray J, DiStefano A, Yang J, Wood M. Displacement and HIV: Factors influencing antiretroviral therapy use by ethnic Shan migrants in Northern Thailand. *Journal of the Association of Nurses in AIDS Care* 2016;27:709–721.

Neal J, Neal Z, VanDyke E, Kornbluh M. Expediting the analysis of qualitative data in evaluation: A procedure for the rapid identification of themes from audio recordings (RITA). *American Journal of Evaluation* 2015;36(1):118–132.

Needle RH, Trotter RT II, Singer M, Bates C, et al. Rapid assessment of the HIV/AIDS crisis in racial and ethnic minority communities: An approach for timely community interventions. *American Journal of Public Health* 2003;93(6):970–979.

Nunns H. Responding to the demand for quicker evaluation findings. *Social Policy Journal of New Zealand* 2009;34:89–99.

Pace R, Pluye P, Bartlett G, et al. Testing the reliability and efficiency of the pilot Mixed Methods Appraisal Tool (MMAT) for systematic mixed studies review. *International Journal of Nursing Studies* 2012;49(1):47–53.

Palinkas L, Zatzick D. Rapid assessment procedure informed clinical ethnography (RAPICE) in pragmatic clinical trials of mental health services implementation: Methods and applied case study. *Administration and Policy in Mental Health and Mental Health Services Research* 2019; https://doi.org/10.1007/s10488–018–0909–3.

Palmer J, Pocock C, Burton L. Waiting, power and time in ethnographic and community-based research. *Qualitative Research* 2017;18(4):416–432.

Park J, Zeanah E. An evaluation of voice recognition software for use in interview-based research: A research note. *Qualitative Research* 2005;5(2):245–251.

Pasco AC, Morse JM, Olson JK. The cross-cultural relationships between nurses and Filipino Canadian patients. *Journal of Nursing Scholarship* 2004;36(3):239–246.

Patmon F, Gee P, Rylee T, Readdy N. Using interactive patient engagement technology in clinical practice: A qualitative assessment of nurses' perceptions. *Journal of Medical Internet Research* 2016;18(11):30–42.

Patton M. *Qualitative Research and Evaluation Methods*. Thousand Oaks: SAGE; 2002.

Pearson A, Jordan Z, Lockwood C, Aromataris E. Qualitative research reporting. *International Journal of Nursing Practice* 2015;21:670–676.

Pearson R. Rapid assessment procedures are changing the way UNICEF evaluates its projects. *Hygie* 1989;8:23–25.

Pearson R, Kessler S. Rapid assessment methodology for evaluation by UNICEF. In: *Rapid Assessment Methodologies: Qualitative Methodologies for Planning and Evaluation of Health-Related Programs*, Scrimshaw N, Gleason R, editors. Boston: International Nutrition Foundation for Developing Countries; 1992.

Petersen LA, Simpson K, Sorelle R, Urech T, Chitwood SS. How variability in the institutional review board review process affects minimal-risk multisite health services research. *Annals of Internal Medicine* 2012;156(10):728–735.

Petro N. Hate taking notes – try mind mapping. *GP Solo* 2010:21–23.

Pink S. Representing the sensory home: Ethnographic experience and anthropological hypermedia. *Social Analysis: The International Journal of Anthropology* 2003; 47(3): 4–63.

Pink S. *Doing Visual Ethnography.* London: SAGE; 2006.

Pink S. Digital–visual–sensory-design anthropology: Ethnography, imagination and intervention. *Arts and Humanities in Higher Education* 2014;13(4):412–427.

Pink S. *Doing Sensory Ethnography.* London: SAGE; 2015.

Pink S, Morgan J. Short term ethnography: Intense routes to knowing. *Symbolic Interactionism* 2013;36(3):351–361.

Pinnock H, Barwick M, Carpenter CR, Eldridge S, Grandes G, Griffiths C, et al. Standards for Reporting Implementation Studies (StaRI) statement. *BMJ* 2017;356:6795.

Polito C, Cribbs S, Martin G, O'Keefe T, Herr D, Rice T, Sevransky J. Navigating the Institutional Review Board approval process in a multicentre observational critical care study. *Critical Care Medicine* 2014;42(5):1105–1109.

Punch S. Hidden struggles of fieldwork: Exploring the role and use of field diaries. *Emotion, Space and Society* 2012;5:86–93.

Rabinow P. Representations are social facts: Modernity and post-modernity in Anthropology. In: *Writing Culture: The Poetics and Politics of Ethnography*, Clifford J, Marcus G, editors. Berkeley: University of California Press; 1986:234–261.

Rapport N. The narrative as fieldwork technique: Processual ethnography for a world on motion. In: *Constructing the Field: Ethnographic Fieldwork in the Contemporary World*, Amit V, editor. London: Routledge; 2000:70–95.

Reddy D. Caught! The predicaments of ethnography in collaboration. In: *Fieldwork Is Not What It Used to Be: Learning Anthropology's Method in a Time of Transition*, Faubion J, Marcus G, editors. Ithaca: Cornell University Press; 2009:89–112.

Reed JE, Card AJ. The problem with Plan-Do-Study-Act cycles. *BMJ Quality & Safety* 2016;25:147–152.

Reid A, Gough S. Guidelines for reporting and evaluating qualitative research: What are the alternatives? *Environmental Education Research* 2000;6(1):59–91.

Reynolds J, Lewis S. Ethnography and evaluation: Temporalities of complex systems and methodological complexity. *Anthropology & Medicine* 2019;26(1):1–17.

Rivoal I, Salazar N. Introduction: Contemporary ethnographic practice and the value of serendipity. *Social Anthropology* 2013;108:178–185.

Roper JM, Shapira J. *Ethnography in Nursing Research.* Thousand Oaks: Sage Publications; 2000.

Rotman D, Preece J, He Y, Druin A. Extreme ethnography: Challenges for research in large scale online environments. iConference 2012, 7–10 February 2012, Toronto, Ontario, Canada.

Sandelowski M, Leeman J. Writing usable qualitative health research findings. *Qualitative Health Research* 2012;22(10):1–10.

Schensul S, Schensul J, LeCompte M. *Essential Ethnographic Methods.* Walnut Creek: AltaMira Press; 1999.

Schneeweiss S, Shrank WH, Ruhl M, Maclure M. Decision-making aligned with rapid-cycle evaluation in health care. *International Journal of Technology Assessment in Health Care* 2015;31:214–222.

Schopper D, Dawson A, Upshur R, et al. Innovations in research ethics governance in humanitarian settings. *BMC Medical Ethics* 2015;16:1–12.

Schopper D, Upshur R, Matthys F, Singh JA, Bandewar SS, et al. Research ethics review in humanitarian contexts: The experience of the independent ethics review board of Medecins Sans Frontieres. *PLoS Medicine* 2009;6:e1000115.

Scott SD, Pollock C. The role of nursing unit culture in shaping research utilization behaviors. *Research in Nursing and Health* 2008;31(4):298–309.

Scott SD, Sharpe H, O'Leary K, Dehaeck U, Hindmarsh K, Moore JG, Osmond MH. Court reporters: A viable solution for the challenges of focus group data collection? *Qualitative Health Research* 2009;19(1):140–146.

Scott K, McMahon S, Yumkella F, Diaz T, George A. Navigating multiple options and social relationships in plural health systems: A qualitative study exploring healthcare seeking for sick children in Sierra Leone. *Health Policy Planning* 2014;29(3):292–301.

Scrimshaw S, Carballo M, Ramos L, Blair B. The AIDS rapid anthropological assessment procedures: A tool for health education planning and evaluation. *Health Education Quarterly* 1991;18(1):111–123.

Scrimshaw S, Hurtado E. Anthropological involvement on the Central American diarrheal disease control project. *Social Science & Medicine* 1988;27(1):97–105.

Scrimshaw S, Hurtado E. *Rapid Assessment Procedures for Nutrition and Primary Health Care: Anthropological Approaches to Improving Programme Effectiveness.* Tokyo: The United Nations University; 1987.

Shaw B, Amouzou A, Miller NP, Tafesse M, Bryce J, Surkan PJ. Access to integrated community case management of childhood illnesses services in rural Ethiopia: A qualitative study of the perspectives and experiences of caregivers. *Health Policy Planning* 2016;31(5):656–666.

Shrank W. The Center for Medicare and Medicaid Innovation's blueprint for rapid-cycle evaluation of new care and payment models. *Health Affairs* 2013;32(4):807–812.

Silberman G, Kahn K. Burdens of research imposed by Institutional Review Boards: The state of the evidence and its implications for regulatory reform. *The Milbank Quarterly* 2011;89(4):599–627.

Silva JH, Olson J. Promoción de salud y calidad de vida en madres de preadolescentes de la comunidad de Chiguayante-Chile: Una etnografía enfocada. *Revista Latino-Americana de Enfermagem* [internet]. 2005;13(spe 2):1164–1168.

Sinden-Carroll L. *Auto-Ethnography in Public Policy Advocacy: Theory, Policy and Practice.* New York: Springer; 2018.

Singh S. Rigour versus timeliness in design studies. *Quality in Research Journal* 2005;5(2):31–40.

Skårås M. Focused ethnographic research on teaching and learning in conflict zones: History education in South Sudan. *Forum for Development Studies* 2018;45:2:217–238.

Skillman M., et al. A framework for rigorous qualitative research as a component of mixed method rapid-cycle evaluation. *Qualitative Health Research* 2019;29(2):279–289.

Smallwood A. Cardiac assessment teams: A focused ethnography of nurses' roles. *British Journal of Cardiac Nursing* 2009;4(3):132–138.

Sobo E. *Culture and Meaning in Health Services Research: An Applied Approach: A Practical Field Guide.* London: Routledge; 2012.

Sonnichsen R. *High Impact Internal Evaluation: A Practitioner's Guide to Evaluation and Consulting Inside Organizations.* Thousand Oaks: Sage; 2000.

Spiers JA, Wood A. Building a therapeutic alliance in brief therapy: The experience of community mental health nurses. *Archives of Psychiatric Nursing* 2010;24(6):373–386.

Spradley J. *Participant Observation.* New York: Holt, Rinehard & Winston; 1980.

Stevens A, Garritty C, Hersi M, Moher D. Developing PRISMA-RR, a reporting guideline for rapid reviews of primary studies (Protocol); 2018. Available from: www.equator-network.org/wp-content/uploads/2018/02/PRISMA-RR-protocol.pdf

Stimson GV, Fitch C, Rhodes T. *The Guide on Rapid Assessment Methods for Drug Injecting.* Geneva: World Health Organisation Programme on Substance Abuse; 1997.

Stimson GV, Fitch C, Rhodes T, Ball A. Rapid assessment and response: Methods for developing public health responses to drug problems. *Drug and Alcohol Review* 1999;18(3):317–325.

Tansey C, Herridge M, Heslegrave R, Lavery JV. A framework for research ethics review during public emergencies. *CMAJ* 2010;182(14):1533–1537.

Tattersall C, Vernon S. Mind mapping as a tool in qualitative research. *Nursing Times* 2007;103(26):32–33.

Taylor B, Henshall C, Kenyon S, Litchfield I, Greenfield S. Can rapid approaches to qualitative analysis deliver timely, valid findings to clinical leaders? A mixed methods study comparing rapid and thematic analysis. *BMJ Open* 2018:e019993.

Tessier S. From field notes to transcripts to tape recordings: Evolution or combination? *International Journal of Qualitative Methods* 2012;11(4):446–460.

Tong A, Sainsbury P, Craig J. Consolidated criteria for reporting qualitative research (COREQ): A 32-item checklist for interviews and focus groups. *International Journal of Quality in Health Care* 2007;19:349–357.

Tricco AC, Langlois EV, Straus SE. Rapid reviews to strengthen health policy and systems: A practical guide. *World Health Organization, Alliance for Health Policy and Systems Research*; 2017. Available at: www.who.int/alliance-hpsr/resources/publications/rapid-review-guide/en/.

Trotter RT, Needle RH. RARE project: Field assessment training methods workbook; 2000. Available from: http://jan.ucc.nau.edu/rtt/pdf%20format%20pubs/Trotter%202000%20pdf%20Pubs/RARE%20Methods%20Resource%20Guide%202000.pdf

Trotter RT, Singer M. Rapid assessment strategies for public health: Promise and problems. In: *Community Intervention and AIDS*, Trickett E, Pequegnat W, editors. New York: Oxford University Press; 2005:130–152.

UNCHR. Real-time evaluations. *Forced Migration Review* 2002;14:43–47.

Utarini A, Winkvist A, Pelto G. Appraising studies in health using rapid assessment procedures (RAP): Eleven critical criteria. *Human Organization* 2001;60(4):390–400.

Van Maanen, J. Commentary: On the matter of voice. *Journal of Management Inquiry* 1996;5(4):375–381.

Van Maanen, J. Ethnography as work: Some rules of engagement. *Journal of Management Studies* 2011;48(1):218–234.

Vannini P, Mosher, H. A question of quality: The art/science of doing collaborative public ethnography. *Qualitative Research* 2013;13(4):428–441.

Vincent N, Allsop S, Shoobridge J. The use of rapid assessment methodology (RAM) for investigating illicit drug use: A South Australian experience. *Drug and Alcohol Review* 2000;19:419–426.

Vindrola-Padros C. Writing against culture in the NHS: Can anthropologists shed new light on how we think about and use 'culture' in the health sector? *Practicing Anthropology* 2016;38(4):21–23.

Vindrola-Padros, C. Looking at the field from afar and bringing it closer to home. In: *Mothering from the Field: The Impact of Motherhood on Site-Based Research,* Muhammad B, Neuilly M, editors. New Brunswick: Rutgers University Press; 2019:76–88.

Vindrola-Padros C. An Introduction to Rapid Qualitative Research, in preparation.

Vindrola-Padros C, Brage E, Johnson GA. Rapid, responsive and relevant? A systematic review of rapid evaluations in healthcare. *American Journal of Evaluation* 2020, doi: 10.1177/1098214019886914.

Vindrola-Padros C, Eyre L, Baxter H, et al. Addressing the challenges of knowledge co-production in quality improvement: Learning from the implementation of the researcher-in-residence model. *BMJ Quality & Safety* 2018;28(1):67–73.

Vindrola-Padros C., Johnson GA. Rapid techniques in qualitative research: A critical review of the literature. *Qualitative Health Research* 2020, doi: 10.1177/1049732320921835.

Vindrola-Padros C, Vindrola-Padros B. Quick and dirty? A systematic review of the use of rapid ethnographies in healthcare organisation and delivery. *BMJ Quality & Safety* 2018;27(4):321–330.

Vindrola-Padros C, Wood V, Swart N, McIntosh M, Morris S, Crowe S, Fulop NJ. The timely sharing of findings: Draft Standards for Rapid Ethnographies and Appraisal Methods (STREAM) in healthcare quality improvement; unpublished manuscript.

von Elm E. The strengthening of the reporting of observational studies in epidemiology (STROBE) statement: Guidelines for reporting observational studies. *Annals of Internal Medicine* 2007;147:573.

Vougioukalou S, Boaz A, Gager M, Locock L. The contribution of ethnography to the evaluation of quality improvement in hospital settings: Reflections on observing co-design in intensive care units and lung cancer pathways in the UK. *Anthropology & Medicine* 2019;26(1):18–32.

Wall, S. Focused ethnography: A methodological adaptation for social research in emerging contexts. *Forum Qualitative Sozialforschung / Forum: Qualitative Social Research* 2014;16(1):Art. 1, http://nbn-resolving.de/urn:nbn:de:0114-fqs150111.

Waring J, Jones L. Maintaining the link between methodology and method in ethnographic health research. *BMJ Quality & Safety* 2016;25(7):556–557.

Warren C. Writing the other, inscribing the self. *Qualitative Sociology* 2000; 23 (2):183–199.

Watkins D. Rapid and rigorous qualitative data analysis: The 'RADaR' technique for applied research. *International Journal of Qualitative Methods* 2017;16:1–9.

Watson TJ. Ethnography, reality, and truth: The vital need for studies of 'how things work' in organizations and management. *Journal of Management Studies* 2011;48 (1):202–217.

Whiteford L, Trotter RT II. *Ethics for Anthropological Research and Practice.* Long Grove: Waveland Press; 2008.

Wholey JS. *Evaluation and Effective Public Management.* Boston: Little Brown; 1983.

Williams H, Kachur P, Nalwamba N, Hightower A, Simoonga C, Mphande P. A community perspective on the efficacy of malaria treatment options for children in Lundazi District, Zambia. *Tropical Medicine and International Health* 1999;4 (10):641–652.

Wilson PM, Petticrew M, Calnan MW, et al. Does dissemination extend beyond publication: A survey of a cross section of public funded research in the UK. *Implementation Science* 2010a;5:61.

Wilson PM, Petticrew M, Calnan MW, et al. Disseminating research findings: what should researchers do? A systematic scoping review of conceptual frameworks. *Implementation Science* 2010b;5:91.

Wolcott HF. *Ethnographic Research in Education.* Washington, DC: American Educational Research Association; 1980.

Wright A, Sittig D, Ash J, et al. Lessons learned from implementing service-oriented clinical decision support at four sites: A qualitative site. *International Journal of Medical Informatics* 2015;84:901–911.

Yardley L. Dilemmas in qualitative health research. *Psychology and Health* 2000;15:215–228.

Zakocs R, Hill JA, Brown P, Wheaton J, Freire KE. The data-to-action framework: A rapid program improvement process. *Health Education & Behavior: The Official Publication of the Society for Public Health Education* 2015;42(4):471–479.

Zarinpoush F, Sychowski SV, Sperling J. *Effective Knowledge Transfer and Exchange: A Framework.* Toronto: Imagine Canada; 2007.

Zatzick D, Rivera F, Jurkovich G, Russo J, Trusz SG, Wang J, et al. Enhancing the population impact of collaborative care interventions: Mixed method development and implementation of stepped care targeting posttraumatic stress disorder and related comorbidities after acute trauma. *General Hospital Psychiatry* 2011;33:123–134.

Index

CPSIA information can be obtained
at www.ICGtesting.com
Printed in the USA
LVHW101059180121
676736LV00008B/6